K. BRYNOLF LYON

Toward a Practical Theology of Aging

Don S. Browning, *editor*

THEOLOGY AND PASTORAL CARE

FORTRESS PRESS
PHILADELPHIA

Library of Congress Cataloging-in-Publication Data

Lyon, K. Brynolf, 1953–

Toward a practical theology of aging.

(Theology and pastoral care)
Bibliography: p.
1. Aged—Religious life. 2. Aging—Religious aspects
—Christianity. 3. Aging. I. Browning, Don S.
II. Title. III. Series: Theology and pastoral care
series.
BV4580.L85   1985   261.8'3426   85–47720
ISBN 0–8006–1735–5

1722F85   Printed in the United States of America   1–1735

For Mary

Contents

Series Foreword

Our purpose in the Theology and Pastoral Care Series is to present ministers and church leaders wth a series of readable books that will (1) retrieve the theological and ethical foundations of the Judeo-Christian tradition for pastoral care, (2) develop lines of communication between pastoral theology and the other disciplines of theology, (3) create an ecumenical dialogue on pastoral care, and (4) do this in such a way as to affirm yet go beyond the recent preoccupation of pastoral care with secular psychotherapy and the other social sciences.

The books in this series are written by authors who are well acquainted with psychology, psychotherapy, and the other social sciences. All of the authors affirm the importance of these disciplines for modern societies and for ministry in particular, but they see them also as potentially destructive of human values unless they are guided in their practical application by tested religious and ethical traditions. But to retrieve the best of the Judeo-Christian tradition for the church's care and counseling is a challenging intellectual task—a task to which few writers in the area of pastoral care have attended with sufficient thoroughness. This series addresses that task out of a broad ecumenical stance, with all of the authors taking an ecumenical approach to theology. Besides a vigorous investigation of Protestant resources, there are specific treatments of pastoral care in Judaism and Catholicism.

We hope that the series will help ministers and church leaders view afresh the theological and ethical foundations of care and counseling. All of the books have a practical dimension, but even more important than that, they help us see care and counseling differently. Compared with writings of the last thirty years in this field, some of the books will seem startlingly different. They will need to be read and pondered with care. But I have little doubt that the series will make a profound and lasting impact upon the way we understand and practice our care for one another.

In *Toward a Practical Theology of Aging,* Brynolf (Bernie) Lyon has accomplished a task that is difficult to conceive and even more difficult to accomplish. He retrieves the ancient traditions on aging that one finds in Western Christianity. In addition, he appropriates them with sufficient philosophical clarity to help guide us not only in our care of the aging but also in our use of the growing body of social science literature on aging. This latter accomplishment is significant. More and more, ministers, doctors, nurses, social workers, and other helping professionals are turning to psychology, human development, and sociology to get oriented in their care of the growing number of aging people in our society. In view of this, the question arises, what can theology contribute? What can we learn from the ancient and not-so-ancient Christian religious traditions about what it means to grow old?

Bernie Lyon argues that there is much that we can learn. Professor Lyon is principally interested in defining the normative question of how humans should age. Or to say it differently, he is interested in what kinds of people we should become when we age. This model (or models) of human fulfillment in aging is important to guide the church's care. It is a matter of determining the goal or goals of the human life cycle and what a practical theology of aging can contribute to the clarification of these goals.

Not only does Professor Lyon mine the riches of the Bible, Greek philosophy, John Chrysostom, John Calvin, and Friedrich Schleiermacher on the meaning of aging, but he also uses these resources to advance a telling critique of the value assumptions of the contemporary social science understandings of aging. Hence, Bernie Lyon helps us use these sciences without unconsciously capitulating to their own normative images of what we should become when we age. I am pleased to recommend this book to all those who are concerned about aging, in other people and in themselves.

DON S. BROWNING

CHAPTER 1

Aging and Human Fulfillment

What is the nature of human fulfillment? The centuries of human thought have known many answers: from the ancient Greek debates over *vita contemplativa* and *vita activa* to the Confucian Knight of the Way, from practical ethical striving to hedonic detachment, from the imitation of Christ to the self-actualizing personality—all interpretations of how human fulfillment should be conceived. The intricate web between the historically given social structure and the contemporary knowledge has yielded diverse answers. It is perhaps merely indicative of that web that to speak of human fulfillment today often evokes images of the urban everyperson meandering from psychotherapist to human potential meeting.

The understanding of human fulfillment in much of contemporary Western popular culture is circumscribed by an excruciating "mental hypochondriasis"—the ironic citadel of less elitist versions of "psychological man."[1] When fulfillment does not specifically mean orgasmic, it often refers to the process of "finding out who one really is"; a task made bearable nowadays by finding out that, after all, it is who one really wants to be anyway. Thus does the *telos* of fulfillment come to be identified with the mastery of "pulling your own strings." Such cheap grace is undoubtedly as disturbing to some as it is appealing to others. But, then, satisfaction is hard to come by, even in an age that worships at its altar.

THE FOCUS

This book enters this arena by virtue of its seeking to develop certain elements of a practical theology of aging.[2] It is *not* a how-to book on pastoral care with the aging and is not a substitute for sensitive reflection on such how-to questions. Yet it is hoped that this discussion will enable a rethinking of certain issues often taken for granted in such books and in such reflection. My purpose is, one might say, to compose a way of life: to develop an image of human fulfillment for the aging with the intention of clarifying certain foundational issues in pastoral care with older adults.

To put it in the form of a question I will ask: What is the nature of human fulfillment in aging? This question is not as esoteric as it might at first sound. It may be found, at least implicitly, in a variety of very public and very private contexts:

- in church committees planning educational, worship, or service programs and experiences for older adults;

- in pastoral counseling and spiritual direction with the elderly;

- in the agonizing search of a middle-aged daughter and her infirm mother as to where the mother is to live now that she can no longer care for herself;

- and in moments, if only fleeting, when the young themselves capture a glimpse of the possibility of their own old age.

In all of these contexts, the question of what human fulfillment can mean in old age forms at least the background of conversation. While the rush of committee work, the emotional intensity of the moment, or the infatuation with a new program or technique may mediate against our recognizing its presence in such contexts, it yet lies only barely beneath the surface.

Raising this question, of course, assumes that it is important to do so. Many who recognize its existence in any or all of the above contexts seem, however, to have little interest in seeking to address it critically. Our question has, it is sometimes said, little or no practical payoff: the *real* questions in pastoral care with older adults are those of learning effective counseling or other programmatic techniques and the appropriate occasions on which to apply them. As our discussion proceeds, I will seek to show the extent to which this position is fundamentally wrongheaded. The interpretation of human fulfillment in aging is not simply an innocuous abstraction; it is rather a dramatically formative lens through which we under-

stand both what is going on in particular situations and the general
direction of what is to be done. The issue is not, therefore, how our
question may be made relevant to pastoral care, but rather how to
reflect critically on what is foundational to our pastoral care.

The explicit focus of this book, however, is but an instance of a
far-broader question: Does the Christian witness really say anything
meaningful to us any longer about what we do in pastoral care? Yet,
this too is but a part of an even-broader question: Is postmodern
practical theology possible? There ought to be little doubt as to the
seriousness of these questions today. Surely it is here, at that
juncture of initiative in our everyday lives which practical theology
takes as its focus, that our interpretations of the Christian witness
must finally find self-critical expression. But it is here also that we
must face the hard questions as to the type of existence made
possible by such interpretations. With respect to our concern with
aging, for example, the time is well past when the issue seemed to be
simply whether we could say anything "biblical" about aging. It is
now whether we can say anything meaningful and anything
adequate both to the Christian witness itself and to the postmodern
character of our existence. While these broader questions cannot be
addressed in any forthright manner here, they yet form the ever-
present counterpoint to our theme.

AN OVERVIEW

To address critically our central question is not an easy task, for
any number of reasons, as we shall see. Since the path we must follow
in attempting this will lead us to not a few distant shores, a brief map
of where we are headed may prove useful to both the experienced
and inexperienced explorers of these regions.

I am proposing a theological interpretation of aging. I will be
suggesting that the Christian community has something important
to say, grounded in its own identity as a community, both to itself and
to the broader world about the meaning of human fulfillment in
aging. While my principal focus in articulating this is on foundational issues in pastoral care with the aging, I believe that many of the
issues to be discussed are also relevant to reflection on religious
education and worship with respect to older adults. As I hope will
become clear as I proceed, however, the discussion is not only about

older adults but about the formation of the community within which individuals age, that is, about us all.

The perspective I will present in these pages is based on two premises. First, our pastoral care needs to be located in the history of Christian discourse on the particular life cycle issues it addresses. We have grown quite proficient at understanding marriage, sexuality, parenthood, aging, etc., in the language of contemporary psychology. We tend, however, to have far greater difficulty grasping what the Christian witness has to say about any of this in a manner that is relevant to the practice of pastoral care. But more than this, we have to a great extent lost a sense of participating in a historic community in pastoral care.[3] The first premise, then, is this: it behooves us to understand that our reflection on most of the issues we face in pastoral care participates in a history of theological reflection *on those issues.*

The second premise is this: while we need to recapture this sense of participating in a history of theological discourse, we do not need to do so uncritically. Recovering a sense of tradition cannot mean pretending we live in the fourth or sixteenth century. It does not mean that we can simply carry forward untransformed the theological discussions of previous eras or naively pretend that the tradition "anticipated" all that is important in our time. Taking the tradition seriously requires, rather, that we think through the claims of the tradition in mutually critical dialogue with contemporary interpretations of experience and the claims of the contemporary theological disciplines.

This essay is an exercise in applying this with respect to the issues of aging. There is, I think, much to be learned both about the tradition itself and about ourselves and our pastoral care in this dialogue. The underlying hope in seeking to do this, at any rate, is that our pastoral care with the aging will be more richly informed for having self-consciously sought to take the tradition seriously. While the sheer magnitude of such an undertaking dooms the discussion at points to idiosyncrasy and oversimplification, the importance of the general thrust of such a project seems to warrant making a beginning.

These two premises suggest the two questions I will be pursuing: (1) What is said about aging in the historic Christian literature? and

(2) Does what is said in that literature make sense *today*? The first question is an extraordinarily complex one because what is said about aging in the historic literature varies widely. Christian theologians, not surprisingly, have not been of one mind about old age. Nonetheless, we can discern some common claims about fulfillment in aging in at least certain important aspects of the theological tradition. I will look briefly at discussions of aging by John Chrysostom, John Calvin, Richard Baxter, and others, in order to illustrate three such claims: (1) old age is a blessing of God, (2) old age is to be a period of growth, and (3) old age is to be marked by a particular religioethical witness.

Not always (handwritten note in right margin)

After suggesting the meaning of these three claims about the nature of fulfillment in aging in the Christian tradition, the problem we must face is whether or not these claims can make sense in our time (and, if so, how). I will seek to place these claims in mutually critical dialogue with contemporary interpretations of aging in the human sciences and with certain contemporary theological positions. This is a difficult and, at times, subtle task. Such is essential, however, if we are to take both our tradition and our contemporary situation seriously.

The principal thematic link in this wide-ranging discussion is what I will call the problem of hope in aging. The problem of hope will arise at several crucial junctures in this discussion. It will arise both as a psychological characteristic and as a limit-dimension of the experience of aging. How we are to make sense of hope in older adulthood, then, will come to be a major question in the latter sections of this discussion.

hope (handwritten note in right margin)

For the church committee member trying to decide if, say, Friendly Visiting is a good thing or not, this may seem like an extraordinarily long way to go. Well, yes, it is. But, as Don Browning has written in an earlier volume in this series, the complexity, diversity, and rapidly changing character of our world sometimes awakens in us the awareness that "we must at least for a moment give up our illusions of life's simplicity, and begin to think in fresh ways, even with regard to such elementary tasks as how to show love for our neighbor."[4] So we begin.

CHAPTER 2

The Cultural Context
of Aging

Respect for the elderly is now a matter of manners divorced from civility. It is no longer a mark of being civilized, but a quaint pathology of what used to be called one's upbringing: a nuisance of the moral sense for certain unhappy straddlers of the technological age. Even to mention this today is to run the risk of sounding reactionary. My point in doing so, however, is not to lament the loss of the Victorian ethos but rather simply to note the obvious: some things have changed.

In this chapter I intend to set the stage for the constructive effort that follows by offering an interpretation of why the question of aging arises at all for us today and why it arises in the way in which it does. This reading of the contemporary cultural context of aging forms the groundwork for our reflections on the context and challenges of thinking about human fulfillment in old age in our time.

THE CHANGING CONTEXT OF AGING

The Fundamental Fact of Aging

The fundamental fact about old age in contemporary society is that it is less and less a rarity. This, perhaps more than anything else, differentiates old age in our time from its historical manifestations. The percentage of the population over sixty-five years of age in this country has increased from less than 2 percent in 1790 to over 11 percent in 1980. Indeed, there are more than 10 million people in this country who are seventy-five years of age and over—a trend which Carl Eisdorfer has referred to as the "aging of the aged."[1] The situation in this country differs from that in the world as a whole, of course, but the general trends are similar. Those trends indicate a growing percentage of the world's population in the older age group.

The fundamental fact about old age gains its real significance not from this purely quantitative reality, however. Rather, its deeper significance lies in the increasing trivialization of old age itself. It must be admitted frankly that old age is rapidly losing whatever scarcity value it once possessed. The majority of the population in this country can, barring nuclear holocaust, realistically *anticipate* living several years in the age classification we call old age. I call this the fundamental fact about aging in contemporary society, then, because the very expectational terrain of our lives now routinely includes an extended period of life as "elderly" people. The "average expectable life cycle," to borrow a phrase from Robert Butler, is itself being fundamentally altered.

As recently as two hundred years ago a young couple could have children and anticipate that one or the other parent would not live to see the youngest child leave home. The "empty nest" period now, however, lasts well over a decade. In other words, a newly married couple can now anticipate that more than a third of their married life will remain after all of their children have left home.[2]

This change is also manifested in work and retirement patterns. The historian David Hackett Fischer has observed that "two hundred years ago scarcely anyone retired in the full modern sense of the word. Most men worked until they wore out."[3] In our time, of course, not only are increasing numbers of people retired, but most younger persons can actually anticipate a period of retirement. Retirement, and the anticipation of it, of course, may be experienced ambivalently. Yet, even that ambivalence is indicative of the shift in our expectational horizons.

There are any number of other ways in which the expectational landscape of our lives is being dramatically altered by this fundamental fact. These changes affect not only individual psychology, but also reach to some of the most basic issues in social interchange. Many moral and political battlelines have already been drawn between social obligation and individual liberty on issues such as social security, health care, and housing. In such a situation, we struggle with the economic and political realities of our pluralistic world to achieve some semblance of coherence and moral rectitude. The challenges raised by the fundamental fact, no longer capable of being seen in isolation or effectively treatable by patchwork solutions, throw us back to an underlying issue with respect to a world growing older—the fundamental ambiguity of aging.

The Fundamental Ambiguity
of Aging

Despite the changes generated by the fundamental fact that old age is more readily attained in contemporary society, at least one thing remains the same: old age continues to be seen as, at best, an ambiguous achievement. Whatever glorious attributes have been ascribed to old age, its underside of loss, physical decline, and nearness to death has never been far from sight. As one examines the historical literature, for example, one may be tempted to suggest a splitting of the negative and positive aspects of aging into the "counsels of resignation" and the "counsels of anticipation." The writings of the counsels of resignation either rage against the unfairness of a strong middle age grown weak or resign themselves to the prospect that—besides suicide or an early death—old age is the only alternative one has. The writings of the counsels of anticipation, on the other hand, see old age if not as the awaited culmination, at least as a valuable and important stage of life.

There is a deeper ambiguity than that simply between the "counsels of resignation" and the "counsels of anticipation," however. Indeed, it is the deeper ambiguity I have in mind when I speak of the fundamental ambiguity of old age. There is, perhaps in all of us, an ambiguity about the aged and the prospect of our own old age that becomes externalized and "split" in the two counsels. In all societies we know this ambiguity has existed. In noting the transhistorical character of this ambiguity, the gerontologist Robert Kastenbaum has ruefully commented: "While reaching a good old age has been a common hope, being old has rarely been anyone's ambition."[4]

There is, as Andrew Achenbaum has remarked, no single cause for this ambiguity. As he put it: "Varied and inconsistent feelings about becoming old, in short, reflect the richness, contradictions, and paradoxes manifest in the human condition."[5] Yet, while there may not be only one cause for the ambiguity, there can be no doubt that our uneasiness with our finitude (and the consequent focusing of this issue on decline and death with respect to aging) is an important dimension of it. In Leo Tolstoy's classic *The Death of Ivan Ilyich* this is poignantly portrayed as Ilyich gradually becomes aware of the reality of his own impending death:

> The example of the syllogism which he had learned in Kiezwetter's *Logic:* "Caius is a man, men are mortal, therefore Caius is mortal," had seemed to him all his life to be true as applied to Caius but certainly not as regards himself. That Caius—man in the abstract—was mortal, was perfectly correct; but he was not Caius nor man in the abstract: he had always been a creature quite, quite different from all others. He had been little Vanya with a mamma and a papa. . . . What did Caius know of the smell of the striped leather ball Vanya had been so fond of? Was it Caius who had kissed his mother's hand like that, and had Caius heard the silken rustle of her skirts? Was it Caius who had rioted like that over the cakes and pastry at the Law School? Had Caius been in love like that?
>
> And Caius was certainly mortal, and it was right for him to die; but for me, little Vanya, Ivan Ilyich, with all my thoughts and emotions— it's a different matter altogether.[6]

The little Vanyas within us all cry out at the starker realities of our finitude. That aging signifies an increasing closeness to death and, perhaps more difficult still, the potentially fragmenting fear of decline intensifies the fundamental ambiguity of growing older.

While our uneasiness with our finitude forms an important dimension of the ambiguity of aging, we are mistaken if we read that ambiguity simply within these terms. The fundamental ambiguity of aging finds its roots as well in the relations of power in the structures of society and in the inevitably ambivalent relations to one's parents.

The Fundamental Problem of Aging

The fundamental fact about old age and the fundamental ambiguity of aging have coalesced with the institutionalization of the study of aging to produce an explosion of interest in old age over the past several years. We have been deluged with studies in the social and psychological sciences concerning the nature of the aging process. Amidst this abundance, however, we are apt to feel a peculiar sense of uneasiness. This is due not only to the sheer quantity of material available for our study but also to the fact that some of our most pressing concerns with respect to aging in our time seem to have gained, until quite recently, little serious attention. Kastenbaum, in lamenting the direction of much contemporary human science literature, holds that the historic question has not been, How do we age? "Rather, it has been the question of practical morality, of applied values: 'How am I to live if my fate is to both age and die?' 'What does life mean if it replaces youth with age?'"[7] The historic approach to the problem of aging better reflects the genuine concerns of the aging. In the daily warp and woof of life, people are not as concerned with the intricate processes of aging as with what sense to make of lives that grow old. Those individuals struggling with the awareness of their own aging may be initially impressed, but not much helped, by finding a litany of statistics and charts in response. The questions to which we have the most readily available answers, it seems, are not the questions to which we most *seek* answers. This, I would suggest, constitutes the central problem in understanding aging today.

The problem, as it manifests itself in our attempts to come to grips with our own aging, is not that much important information cannot be gleaned from the human science literature. The problem, rather, is that we have few serious frameworks within which that information could find its proper place in response to our deepest questions. The frameworks we do have are often rough-hewn amalgamations of platitudes, moralisms, and uncritically appropriated facts and theories. Too often we must confront our own aging and the aging of others with bromides concocted at the last moment—mixtures frequently undigestible in face of the real threats to the aging self.

This problem is also acute for those who care for the aged— ministers, nurses, social workers, psychotherapists, doctors, etc. Without a coherent overarching framework or orientation, techniques for helping can rapidly degenerate into a profoundly relativistic technologism.[8] Held together by no more than the flimsy bands of an "enlightened" eclecticism, our disjointed techniques threaten the very ground beneath our feet. When we take the time to wonder what ground we do have—what vision of human fulfillment in aging really operates in our helping—we often realize that we have no more than the uncritically appropriated value-slants of certain human science theories, a naive theologism, or an un-examined "personal experience."

This problem should not, however, be seen as an isolated confusion peculiar to our reflection on aging. It quite clearly mirrors a broader sociocultural theme. As the philosophers Jurgen Habermas, Hans-Georg Gadamer, Hannah Arendt, and Richard Bernstein have observed, contemporary culture tends to treat nearly all practical questions as questions of technical rationality.[9] Value questions either go unrecognized, are seen as outside the domain of rational discourse altogether (and, therefore, seen as demanding a purely subjective, decisional solution), or are treated only in their technological aspects (whereby the implicit value-character of technology itself supplants the complexities and depth of the underlying value question).

In a culture in which the justification of values has been removed to the private sphere of the individual, the question of human fulfillment in old age cannot but appear impositional when it arises in the public forum. Yet, the question inevitably and necessarily arises in the public forum.[10] Thus, it seems to many today that if that question is to avoid an encroaching moralism, it can only be answered within the terms of "doing your own thing" or "pulling your own strings." That these responses to such deeply experienced questions are vapid and disintegrative of public life is of little effective consequence if one thinks no alternative exists. The resulting problem, though, is that certain less-barren images of fulfillment in old age which inform some public policy and some of the work of pastoral care and the helping professions must often remain submerged in the guise of value-free science or administrative programmatics, thereby excluding what has obvious public import from truly public discussion. This suppression or displacement of the question does not, of course, erase our existential concern, but rather often cripples our ability to address it appropriately and effectively.

In the era of "psychological man," this problem often takes a particularly peculiar form: the question of human fulfillment is transformed into a question of therapeutic efficacy. In a culture permeated with the current therapeutic ethos, however, the obvious moral structure of any notion of "efficacy" is read as a problem of technical rather than practical reason. The manipulation of the self thus finds its end in "psychological man's" poetics of "satisfaction." Since within the confines of the therapeutic ethos, the particular value-slant of "satisfaction" appears self-justifying, the problem is not that of practical reflection, but of the manipulation of the self. The psychological sections of mass-market bookstores—the Daltons, Crowns, and Waldens of our lives—provide ample evidence of this state.

TWO CASE STUDIES OF THE PROBLEM OF MEANING FOR AGING

The Church Life Committee

Given the entrenched character of this general problem, two brief cases may help to illustrate the issues. Think, for example, about this situation.

During a budget planning meeting of the Church Life Committee of a large metropolitan church in the northeastern United States, some committee members expressed a concern about the lack of programming for older members of the congregation. Recognizing that a growing percentage of their church members were in their old age, they suggested beginning a special ministry with the aging. When asked what they were interested in doing and how much money they would need, the committee members talked readily about their interest in such programs as Meals on Wheels, Friendly Visiting, and growth and sharing groups specially designed for the aged. When they were asked to define their overall goals, however, they were far less clear. Some said the goal should be to mediate God's love by enabling older adults to cope more effectively with loss and decline. Some thought the goal should be to encourage the elderly's participation in the life of the church and increase their interaction with others. Others said the major thrust should be to uplift the self-esteem of the aged.

The question this committee found themselves asking, in effect, was what the church's mission and witness ought to be with respect to aging. They were far more prepared to discuss specific programming possibilities than overall goals, however, and even somewhat better prepared to discuss overall goals than to discuss what the Christian witness had to do with any of this. This is not to say that there were not implicit answers to these latter two questions, but rather that they had not really been given much thought. Our interpretations of human fulfillment in aging often form the *background* of conversation in such situations, but are seldom made explicit.

We should not be terribly surprised at this. Since we presume that "good deeds" are central to the life of faith, we sometimes proceed unreflectively on the moral and theological dimensions of the issues we address and move ahead to the nuts and bolts of the technical and programmatic concerns. Yet, this may lead to problems: for example, when disputes about technical procedures conceal more fundamental divergence with regard to moral or theological issues, or when we lose sight of the initiating ground of our procedures or techniques in our efforts to express the Christian witness, or when such procedures come to express understandings of life that cannot be justified by an adequate interpretation of the Christian witness. The press of committee work often does not allow us time to think through these concerns thoroughly. But they do not go away: their presence is reflected in the decisions we reach even on such mundane matters as to what the central challenges of aging are and what "appropriate coping" with those challenges means.

The Case of George and Betty Anderson

A further illustration of the issues involved in aging is provided in this case.

Reverend John Williams was the pastor of a small urban church. He was approached in his study one day by an elderly couple, George and Betty Anderson, who had been lifelong members of the congregation. Until the previous two years, the Andersons had been leaders in the congregation. In Rev. Williams's study, the Andersons said that something had been troubling them for several weeks. George began by saying that they had been thinking about moving to a retirement community in another state. He said that they felt such a move might allow them to associate with more people their own age as well as to enjoy the many recreational benefits the community offered. Betty, however, mentioned that they were concerned about leaving their family, friends, and church after so many years. Moving would be such an upheaval, she said, since they had lived all their lives in the city. George wondered whether they didn't have an obligation to stay near their family, friends, and church. They felt a conflict, however, between—what seemed to them like—a life of continued service and a life of increased enjoyment and relaxation.

Rev. Williams responded by saying that he had, in fact, noticed that they had not been as active in the life of the church recently and he wondered whether that might not be a sign of a growing wish to move. George apologized for their lack of participation, but said that maybe Rev. Williams was right in attributing it to a growing wish to move. Rev. Williams then remarked on how they had both been valuable members of the church, good parents, and hard workers in the community. He wondered aloud whether perhaps they had reached an age when they should take an active step toward enjoying their own lives more. Wasn't it time they thought more about themselves? Since, he said, even God rested on the seventh day, maybe they too should relieve themselves of some of their responsibilities and enjoy the years God had laid before them at this point. He assured them that their presence would be missed in the church, but that the congregation would rejoice in their new life together.

There are any number of things we could wonder about in this pastoral care situation. One of the first things that is likely to strike us, of course, is Rev. Williams's stance toward the Andersons. There can be little doubt that, though many of his remarks were phrased in questions, he had a particular sense of what was the proper thing to do for the Andersons. Rev. Williams clearly had his hand to their backs, pushing them out of his office, the church, and the community. This is all the more distressing since we might well wonder whether Rev. Williams ever really found out why the couple was in his office in the first place. He seems to have assumed that what they wanted was pastoral reassurance of the rightness of the move. Responding on the belief that the Andersons merely wanted to have their guilt assuaged (and that assuaging their guilt was a proper response on his part), Rev. Williams responded to that half of their dilemma. Yet we certainly ought to wonder whether simple pastoral reassurance was in fact the point of the visit. We—and Rev. Williams—will never know. While an overburdened pastor might well project his own wishes for more leisure into this type of situation, there is no way to know from this dialogue what the Andersons themselves might have wanted.

My point in mentioning this case, however, is not to discuss the many issues of counseling procedure which it raises, but rather to use it to look at the image of fulfillment in old age which it implies. While Rev. Williams was hardly conscious of this image at the time, reflection on his part after the fact disclosed its presence to him. Such reflection did not come easily to Rev. Williams. The real question, he said, was not his image of fulfillment, but rather how to help the couple "go ahead and do what they surely wanted to do." Rev. Williams failed to understand, however, that the image of fulfillment he in fact held set the context for what he would "see" with respect to the Andersons.

The dominant image surrounding Rev. Williams's remarks might be said to be sabbath—old age as a period of withdrawal from the responsibilities one has carried out throughout one's earlier life. It was not just any sabbath Rev. Williams had in mind in his encouragement of the Andersons moving, however, it was a sabbath of self-enjoyment and relaxation. Even sabbath has its responsibilities, albeit from Rev. Williams's remarks one might gather that these are principally responsibilities toward oneself. Rev. Williams, in effect, joins the couple in their perception of a conflict between a "life of continued service" and a "life of increased enjoyment." This is particularly remarkable since Rev. Williams does not hold such a position with respect to any other life period. The implication here, of course, is that the moral character of the life cycle shifts rather dramatically from promoting the good-for-others in middle adulthood to promoting the good-for-self in old age. Middle adulthood is marked morally by a self-transcending focus, whereas old age is to be a period of ethical egoism.

This ethical posture, in Rev. Williams's view, however, is grounded in a particular understanding of the process of aging. Old age, he believes, is not only a period of turning inward, but also one of disengagement from society. Having read a few things about "disengagement theory" in his seminary days, he feels that older people tend to adjust better to the losses of aging if the mutual withdrawal between themselves and society can be eased.

It is basically this vision of human fulfillment in old age that operates partly consciously, partly unconsciously in Rev. Williams's interaction with the Andersons. To what extent is this understanding justifiable? Is the image of sabbath an appropriate representation of things central to the Christian witness with respect to aging? Is his understanding of the moral character of old age appropriate and meaningful? Does he correctly understand the central challenges of growing older? All of these questions would need to be addressed in any critical appraisal of his image of fulfillment.

CULTURE AND THE MEANING
OF OLD AGE

There are some who would suggest that while to examine Rev. Williams's interpretation of human fulfillment in old age may be an interesting exercise, it misses the point. In other words, the problem lies not in some abstract image, but rather in the psychodynamic features of Rev. Williams's own life. There is, of course, a good bit of truth in this. The hermeneutics of suspicion (Freud and Marx, for example) have taught us much about the ways in which such interpretations reflect psychological and material dynamics. Yet Rev. Williams was not working in a vacuum. He himself felt that his understanding of old age ought to be publicly defensible. Indeed, his understanding draws on certain facts, theories, and images that the culture itself makes available. There can be no doubt that Rev. Williams appropriated those culturally available elements in his own way, given the psychological structure of his life and the institutional context of his work. The culturally available elements set a particular context for appropriation, however, and we are not mistaken, I believe, to argue that those elements require reflection in themselves. This is not to say that we need not be concerned about the mode of appropriation or the ways in which these elements may be, in Habermas's phrase, systematically distorted. Rather, it is to say that we need to be concerned about both content and dynamic precipitants or, if you will, both reasons and causes in the examination of that broader context.

Rev. Williams has no doubt that the Andersons are older people; more specifically, he has no doubt that they are in their "old age." What he has less sense of, however, is that "old age" is a sociocultural appellation—a conceptual abstraction we use to designate certain things about the life course in society. Thus, for example, when old age begins and what it designates have varied somewhat both across cultures and through history within cultures. Yet to demarcate a particular period of life as "old age" is always to denote more than simply that so many years have passed. Divisions of the life course always carry a social meaning: a certain set of social expectations concerning both the substantive and the functional character of life shape our understanding of the divisions of the human life cycle.

In our society, "old age" takes on its peculiarly modern sense with the discovery of old age as a "social problem" toward the end of the last century. That the aged have problems requiring attention and ameliorative action on the part of the society at large extends at least to the founding of the *gerocomia* (old-age homes) of the eastern Roman Empire. Yet, old age *itself* as a social problem, as Gerald Gruman has noted, took on a particular modern tone with the closing of the frontier and the emergence of the instrumental ethos in the mid- to late nineteenth century.[11] The social meaning of old age changed even further with the establishment of a mandatory retirement age and government-sponsored pension and relief programs.

Many contemporary commentators have suggested, paradoxically, that the peculiarly contemporary meaning of old age is precisely its lack of substantive meaning. David Stannard, for example, has suggested that old age in this country is now a "liminal" period, that is, a period of life without socially prescribed status, roles, or functions.[12] Some have argued, however, that even though old age, as a period of life, now generally lacks socially prescribed status and particular life cycle norms, this does not necessarily mean that it lacks meaning. Rather, they argue, it may come to suggest the pluralization of that meaning itself. Thus, when people speak about the coming "age-irrelevant" society in this country, at least part of what they refer to is the coming plurality of possible life styles that may be socially acceptable in old age. The culture would no longer legitimate only one mode of life in old age, but rather would open the later years to a multiplicity of modes. What we are to make of this, however, is a difficult matter.

On the one hand, the potential pluralization of the meaning of old age is a reflection of our increasing differentiation of the life cycle category "old age." Psychologically, for example, we have learned much about what Robert Butler has called the "facade of chronological age"—the variability of psychological dynamics, cognitive and physical capabilities, and needs of people who fall within a given chronological age range. Culturally, this is reflected in the demand for the loosening of social age-constraints on behavior. Politically, this is reflected in recent federal government policy seeking ways to alter criteria of federal assistance for the aged from solely age-based standards to need-based standards (for example, the "frail elderly" or the "truly needy").

This legitimation of pluralism with respect to life in old age is, then, at least in part, a recognition of the vitality, richness, and strength that can arise from a pluralistic situation. While such recognition is to be welcomed, we must not lose sight of the fact that all such cultural movements are inherently ambiguous. For example, the movement toward an age-irrelevant society is sometimes defended in such a way not only to recognize the psychological and moral importance of individuality, but also to rest upon a normative individualism. In other words, it sometimes entails the collapse of the meaning of old age into the private sphere. This is a part of the more general problem of the truncation of public life in our time and, while it affects those of all ages, it has—as I will later suggest—particularly devastating effects for older adults.

This evacuation of the public meaning of aging cannot exist for very long. Indeed, it can probably only "exist" at all as an ideological masking of the unconscious bonds holding the community together. Even a contractual mode of association stripped to its barest minimum—on which a community bereft of most substantive, shared public meanings is often said to depend—inevitably implicates a deeper (though unarticulated) bond.[13] Thus, however much we should welcome the idea of an age-irrelevant society in many respects, it does not and cannot relieve us of those shared meanings on which the culture and the individual life cycle depend. The task in such a situation, however, becomes one of articulating an interpretation of human fulfillment in old age that can incorporate the wisdom of pluralism without thereby leading to the privatization of the meaning of old age. This, I suggest, forms the context for a practical theological understanding of old age today.

The general problems Rev. Williams and the Church Life Committee face in seeking to interpret the meaning of human fulfillment in old age in our time are not unique to them or their religious context. Certain of the resources they might bring to this discussion are, however, pushed to the forefront given the particularities of the religious communities in which they participate and the faith which informs their identities. The challenge of a nonisolationist pluralism, though, is to think through these particularities in public discussion and in mutually critical dialogue with other participants in this cultural conversation. We often err on either side of this: either insulating our interpretations of the Christian witness from the claims of truly public discussion or effectively abandoning the Christian witness in the face of what may seem to be more culturally central options. Holding a death grip on particular formulations of the Christian witness, however, does not make them true nor does a too-easy incorporation of the spirit of the age. How, then, are we to proceed?

CHAPTER 3

Aging and the Christian Theological Tradition

This essay, as I have said, is a composing of a way of life—a rendering of human fulfillment with aging with the intention of clarifying certain foundational issues in pastoral care with older adults. The irony in this, of course, is that it suggests the necessity of doing precisely what pastoral care has found increasing uneasiness doing: clearly articulating (and, in some cases, even admitting that they exist) those images of human fulfillment that underlie its work. For those who have not exiled themselves to those "reservations of the spirit" supposedly insulated from the broader demands of public life and public discourse, this problem is often experienced particularly acutely.

The problem here is that the individual engaged in pastoral care performs her activity in the context of re-presenting the church's mission and witness. From one perspective, our effort to articulate an interpretation of human fulfillment in aging is precisely an attempt to reflect critically on a certain foundational dimension of the church's mission and witness with respect to aging. Paradoxically, however, the demands of care are more and more perceived as in dynamic conflict with the church's mission and witness. As we discover the limits of human change, the plurality of ways people have of effectively actualizing important wants and needs, and our subsequent reticence at calling sinful or immoral a variety of ways of life previously understood as such, the problem of giving determinate sense to "the church's mission and witness" is compounded as it relates to pastoral care. In such a situation those of us engaged in pastoral care seem confronted with two unhappy alternatives: living a defensively militant propheticism or quietly allowing our pastoral identity to languish in the backwater of our practice. If neither a naive traditionalism nor an abandonment of tradition seems a particularly appealing prospect, however, how are we to proceed?

The first step, I would suggest, is to interpret what, historically, persons reflecting on the Christian witness have said about aging. This is not the final step, but the first one. Even as a first step this is likely to strike some as not terribly obvious, for the history of Christian reflection on such issues in pastoral care has found little place (and certainly no systematic place) in our thinking. While many of the methodological issues that come to play cannot be discussed in this space, it is a relatively entrenched problem and so a few additional comments are perhaps in order.

The history of old age is receiving increased attention today. Surprisingly little has been done, however, with respect to the history of old age in the Christian theological tradition. While there is an ever-increasing number of discussions of old age from the perspective of an interpretation of the Christian witness, there is almost no historical situating of these discussions in terms of the theological tradition *on aging*. What discussions of this historical literature exist have arisen primarily within the context not of the practical theological literature on aging, but of the more general cultural histories. Of course, whether this situation strikes one as particularly lamentable or not depends upon what one thinks practical theology is and how it ought to go about its task.

Indeed, while I think this situation is regrettable, it is nonetheless thoroughly understandable: it derives, in part, out of what Alastair Campbell and others refer to as the applicational model of practical theology. The applicational model of practical theology sees its task as the simple application of a contemporary systematic or dogmatic theology to whatever practical issues arise. What matters from this perspective is not what theologians historically might have had to say about aging, but rather what is now being said about the more general theological symbols, which can then be applied to old age. Practical theology has frequently been more interested in the history of the psychological and sociological traditions than in the history of the Christian tradition.

The problem in this is not with the use of the human sciences themselves, but rather with the lack of interest in what thinking

Christians at any time other then the present moment have had to say about the topic under discussion. While I disagree with the way he sometimes seems to want to make use of the historical literature, I think Thomas Oden is quite right to lament its loss—for all practical purposes—in contemporary discussion in practical theology.[1] An example may help to clarify this.

The theologian Martin J. Heinecken writes, for instance: "There is no special theology for the aging. There is only the one biblically and confessionally based theology which is applied to the problems of older adults."[2] Or, as he put it in another place: "The basic Christian theological affirmations are to be applied to the specific questions that arise in connection with aging and the aged."[3] Heinecken's intention in this, of course, is to maintain the unity of theology, that is, there are not different theologies for different "problems." Whatever one might think of this as a general theological proposition, it encourages seeing the interpretation of the "problems" of aging and the "questions that arise with aging" merely as illustrative material; that is, the interpretation of the problems of older adults serves only as the medium for the application of (an interpretation of) theological doctrine. On a more general level, this approach has often tended to mean two things: (1) it denied interpretations of the experience of aging any critical role in relation to theology, and (2) it effectively cut off attributing any significance to the historic Christian discussion of aging itself.

In such a situation, however, the question arises as to what the point would be in seeking to recover the tradition of Christian discourse on old age for contemporary, constructive practical theology. Two points should be noted about this. First, practical theologians (and especially those concerned with pastoral care) have often found themselves reflecting in a historical vacuum. Without a sense of participating in a history of discourse on particular issues, much of the literature implies (if only by omission) that no theologian had ever thought of addressing the issue before. To a certain extent, of course, this simply reflects what Christopher Lasch refers to as the loss of a sense of history in the general culture.[4] "Tradition" in our time often means no more than the last fad. This is a problem in the truncation of identity as much as anything else. The attempt to recover the tradition of Christian discourse on aging, therefore, has a moral point as well as a hermeneutic one: it is an effort to involve us in a dimension of that practical-moral conversational history that, in part, forms our culture and, thus, ourselves.

Second, however, disregard for the tradition fails to appreciate that the interpretation of the past contains the grounds upon which a critical reworking of the present must be forged. My point here is not that we must simply reaffirm what, for example, John Chrysostom or John Calvin had to say about aging. The practical theological task is not, as I will later make clear, just to find quotations from Cotton Mather or Jerome with which we can agree. Rather, the recovery of the tradition for the purposes of constructive practical theology implies the critical, transformative interpretation of tradition in the contemporary situation. It is to disengage the strangely alien/familiar ground of the past from the "prejudices" of the present so that both the present and the past may be critically rethought.

The immediate problem we face in this, given the virginal character of this territory, is how to proceed. A complete survey of interpretations of aging in the Christian tradition is beyond both my own scope and the scope of this essay. This being the case, I have chosen to offer a tentative interpretation of what I believe may be seen as three fundamental claims of at least certain important aspects of the historic Christian tradition with respect to aging. Two caveats much be noted about this, however. First, I am not claiming that this is the only way (or even the only fruitful way) to read the tradition. There are as many different strands in the understanding of old age in the theological tradition as there are in the understanding of anything else in that tradition. The three claims I will be discussing arise in widely divergent intellectual and social contexts and, thus, make any notion of *the* Christian understanding of aging simple nonsense. Second, as an interpretation of the tradition, the focusing ideas I am offering rest primarily with the attempt to discern a certain structural similarity in many theological discussions of old age. The point even here, of course, is not that there are not other ways to organize the material. The point, rather, is that at least this way of organizing them may help us toward a fruitful contemporary practical theology of aging. Thus, I offer this interpretation not to try to close discussion, but rather to illustrate the way in which a change in context for the discussion might fruitfully proceed.

The three fundamental claims I will discuss in this chapter are: (1)

old age as a blessing, (2) aging as a process of growth, and (3) the religioethical witness of age. These three claims are not independent of one another, but rather interconnect to form a particular understanding of human fulfillment with aging. Roughly, the structure of that understanding is this: fulfillment with aging, as a blessing of God, is a period of growth and this growth is manifested in the religioethical witness of age. In the remainder of this chapter, I will seek to show what this means and to illustrate certain of the ways in which this understanding of fulfillment in old age has been filled out and made determinant. In the following chapters I will ask if this understanding can be reconceptualized so as to form a viable context for pastoral care with the aging in the contemporary world.

OLD AGE AS A BLESSING

The Dominant Tradition

The Christian theological tradition has historically tended to understand old age as a blessing of God. What the idea of blessing has meant precisely has varied considerably, however. At times the idea of blessing seems to refer to age as a reward for virtuous living. The scriptural appeal in this, rightly or wrongly, is frequently to Prov. 16:31: "A hoary head is a crown of glory; it is gained in a righteous life." At other times, the idea of blessing seems to refer to age as a special category in the created order. In this more narrow sense, old age is a special, created good that is due honor and veneration. The scriptural appeal here was often to Lev. 19:32: "You shall rise up before the hoary head, and honor the face of an old man, and you shall fear your God: I am the Lord."

There are various other gradations in the idea of blessing and various other scriptural reference points. In most cases, though, the authority for the claim of the blessing of age also rested upon a general cultural tradition. Thus, many theologians have cited not only Scripture, but also "natural reason" to support this claim. In many sociocultural settings in which Christian theologians have historically written, it was simply self-evident (at least on the level of the "official" cultural norms) that old age was a blessing.

Yet, the idea that old age is a blessing has always been in some tension with both the potentiality of physical/mental deterioration with aging and the religioethical "condition" in which some aged individuals were to be found. On the one hand, then, there has always been tension in claiming that old age is a blessing and yet is subject to potentially severe physical and/or cognitive weakening. As the American Puritan theologian William Bridge captured (perhaps unwittingly) this ambiguity: "Though your infirmities be ever so many and great, yet you have a peculiar honor that is twisted with your infirmity, for it is called the crown of age."[5] Many theologians, therefore, have found themselves on considerably lengthy paths— with not a few imaginative leaps along the way—to carry off the claim.

On the other hand, theologians have been at pains to point out that while old age is a blessing of God, not necessarily all aged persons are of the virtuous variety. As Ambrose put it: "It is not the old age of years which is entitled to praise, but that of deeds."[6] Cotton Mather makes the same point with somewhat more vehemence:

> It is promised as a great blessing to live near an hundred years; but if a man be a sinner at that age, his age will be but a curse upon him. . . . Such a wretched old man must not only perish, but also go down to the Pit with heavier loads of confusion and vexation than those that had not lived so long.[7]

The problem here, of course, is that if old age is a blessing of God, why is it that there are unsavory older people? To turn a popular phrase, why do good things happen to bad people? The theological task was both to uphold the claim concerning old age as a blessing and, at the same time, to argue that the blessing of old age could be subverted or negated by the actions of humans; that is, that it need not necessarily be a sign of virtue.

Given the classical conception of God that undergirded many of these arguments, this was frequently a precarious road. There were two interrelated approaches to this problem. One approach was to claim that "old age" does not refer strictly or primarily to a chronological period of life, but rather to something else: used pejoratively, it referred to a spiritual decline antithetical to the Christian life; in its more frequent positive usage, it referred to special qualities of virtuous individuals of whatever chronological age. A second approach was to claim that the blessing of age was conditional on fulfilling the covenantal requirements.

In order to examine how this claim actually was worked out in a particular case, and how this claim was integrated into a general vision of fulfillment in old age, I have chosen to present Calvin's understanding of aging. As will be seen, Calvin's understanding of old age strains to the very limit the idea that aging is a blessing. Yet, in many respects, it appropriately reflects the tensions that have frequently arisen.

Calvin

In his commentary on Lev. 19:32, Calvin states that "it is a natural law in the hearts of all to reverence and honor old men."[8] He continues: "Many old men, indeed, either by their levity or lewdness or sloth, subvert their own dignity; yet although grey hairs may not always be accompanied by courteous wisdom, still, in itself, age is venerable, according to God's command."[9] These remarks might lead one to believe that Calvin has a rather high estimation of old age. Indeed, in his exposition of the Fifth Commandment in the *Institutes of the Christian Religion,* Calvin says that a long and blessed life is promised to those who honor their father and mother as proof of the favor of God. The present life, even in old age, is to be counted "among the blessings we receive from God."[10]

Despite all of this, Calvin was none too fond of old age. Of course, Calvin was none too fond of human nature in general, either. As regards aging, Calvin shared the widely held prejudice that middle adulthood—that period of life between childhood and old age—was the best period of life. As he wrote, "the middle and manly age is the full age of human life."[11] The difficulty that arises from this position is how one is to understand the stages on either side of the "middle and manly age." Our problem, of course, is with old age and Calvin seems to leave little doubt about his assessment. In his commentary on Eph. 4:13, for example, Calvin argues: "No mention is made of old age for in the Christian progress no place for it is found. Whatever becomes old has a tendency to decay; but the vigor of this spritual life is continually advancing."[12] There could seem to be no more forthright statement contradicting his claim that old age is a blessing. Indeed, this impression only gains added strength from his claim that "it is on account of our sins that we grow old and lose our strength."[13] Calvin writes: "To our sins, therefore, it ought to be imputed that we are liable to diseases, pains, old age, and other inconveniences; for we do not permit Christ to possess us fully, and have not advanced so far in newness of life as to lay aside all that is old." [14] Before concluding, however, that Calvin probably encouraged the stoning of his aged Genevan parishioners, we must briefly place this discussion within the broader context of his interpretation of the Christian life in general.

The Christian life for Calvin is seen from the perspective of the imitation of Christ. Indeed, God has provided Christ as that supreme "pattern we ought to express in our life." The imitation of Christ is no matter of blind or mechanistic imitation, however. As Calvin writes: "It is a doctrine not of the tongue, but of life."[15] Calvin does not, of course, call Christian only those who are perfected in the imitation of Christ—"since no one is found who is not far removed from it."[16] However, Calvin does invoke a key interpretive image for the correct ordering of the Christian life: we must make continual progress in this life toward that goal. The Christian life, then, is one of constant striving to embody the character of Christ which is, nonetheless, an unrealizable goal in earthly life. The final salvation is, most assuredly, otherworldly here, but this in no way lessens the requisites of duty in this life.

Calvin's *Commentaries* provides a recapitulation and extension of the theme of growth. It is suggested there that Christian maturity must be sought in Christ "for full manhood is found in Christ; for foolish men do not, in a proper manner, seek their perfection in Christ. Whoever is a man in Christ is in every respect a perfect man."[17] Maturity is sought, therefore, in this continual advancement toward the ideal. We must, Calvin notes, be constantly advancing "throughout the whole course of our life" toward that "perfect manhood" which is revealed to us in Christ.

Another aspect of Calvin's interpretation of the Christian life that is important for our discussion is the place of suffering or "bearing the cross." Calvin argues:

For whomever the Lord has adopted and deemed worthy of his fellowship ought to prepare themselves for a hard, toilsome life, crammed with very many and various kinds of evil. It is the Heavenly Father's will thus to exercise them so as to put his own children to a definite test.[18]

Humans are prideful, arrogant, boastful beings and the way God has chosen to chasten and, at least potentially, lead toward redemption this sinful creature is through suffering. Through suffering we may be led to recognize our true nature, to set aside the things of the flesh, and to turn our trust to God.

Thus, Calvin argues that God "afflicts us either with disgrace or poverty, or bereavement, or disease, or other calamities" to lead us to the only fount of true and secure trust and hope—Godself.[19] Yet suffering is not to be seen simply as good in and of itself in Calvin's view. As Wilhelm Niesel has acutely noted of Calvin's position: "Misfortune and sorrow in themselves do not help man. They are rather to be seen as punishment for man's alienation from his Creator. If suffering contributes to our salvation it is only because we are in communion with the Son of God."[20] Suffering is, first of all, punishment, of course, but it may also strengthen our relationship with God by reminding us of the futility of our inevitably inordinate love of the present life. Thus, "the Lord instructs his followers in the vanity of the present life by continual proof of its miseries."[21] Calvin is convinced that "the mind is never seriously aroused to desire and ponder the life to come unless it is previously imbued with contempt for the present life."[22] This does not mean, Calvin insists, that the present life is to be despised in all respects, for it is a blessing of God. We are to have contempt but no hatred of it. There is, one might say, a rather fine distinction being made here.

With this brief background in mind, we must return to Calvin's most forthrightly negative statement concerning old age: "No mention is made of old age for in the Christian progress no place for it is found. Whatever becomes old has a tendency to decay; but the vigor of this spiritual life is continually advancing."[23] Calvin's point in saying this, I would argue, is not to suggest that aged persons can no longer participate in the Christian life. Indeed, I would suggest that it is an affirmation of the particular kind of fulfillment he sees in old age. Calvin is primarily using "old age" in a pejorative rather than a strictly chronological sense. The juxtaposition here is between spiritual vigor and bodily decline. The meaning of old age in the

Christian life, Calvin is suggesting, must be understood in terms of the Christian life in general—that is, in terms of "youth" and spiritual vigor rather than in terms of bodily decay. This spiritual emphasis is quite consistent with his commitment to the process of continual growth throughout the life of the Christian.

This interpretation gains some support from Calvin's analysis of Ps. 92:12–15. Calvin suggests there that those who follow the Christian life "continue to flourish and partake of a life which is spiritual and everlasting." He continues: "It is in this sense that he [the psalmist] speaks of their still budding forth and being fat, even in old age, when the natural sap and juices are generally dried up."[24] Calvin concludes:

> It is thus that Jacob, speaking of the great renovation which should take place in the Church, mentions that at that happy period he who was an hundred years old should be a child, meaning that, though old age naturally tends to death, and one who has lived a hundred years is upon the very borders of it, yet in the kingdom of Christ a man would be reckoned as being merely in his childhood, and starting in life, who entered upon a new century. This could be verified in the sense, that after death we have another existence in heaven.[25]

Once again, the juxtaposition is principally between bodily decay and spiritual vigor rather than simply middle adulthood and old age. All this is not meant to disregard Calvin's preference for the "prime of life" in the middle years, but it is meant to suggest that Calvin does provide a basis for an understanding of fulfillment in old age and a means of understanding his claim that old age is a blessing.

Even acknowledging this, Calvin's image of old age does take on a peculiarly negative tone. It does so, I would argue, precisely because of his general interpretation of Christian life—with the addition of one important assumption: old age in and of itself, for Calvin, *is* suffering. Calvin was certainly not alone in this estimation. As one historian has observed of most writers on the subject in that period: "Most writings addressed to the aged took it for granted that their readers were persons to whom life had become a burden."[26] Given Calvin's broader interpretation of suffering in general, though, this stance leads to unique results. Thus, as suffering old age is, on the one hand, justly inflicted punishment for our sins (therefore, his statement that "it is on account of our sins that we grow old and lose our strength"). On the other hand, as suffering it may potentially help the believer in the right ordering of the Christian life (therefore, the emphasis on the possibilities of spiritual growth in old age). This dual emphasis resulting from the interpretation of aging as a type of suffering may serve simply to highlight Calvin's apparently contradictory statement that old age is a blessing and is, indeed, venerable per se. Yet, Calvin's claim that old age is a blessing must be placed within the context of his more general claim that this life, filled with tribulation and suffering as it is, must be counted among the blessings we receive from God. It must be clearly admitted, though, that his position on old age is certainly as conceptually ambiguous on this point as is his claim that we are to have contempt but no hatred for our earthly life.

From what has been suggested so far it should be apparent that fulfillment in old age for Calvin is intimately tied to his general conception of the nature of the Christian life. But old age underscores one particular element: hope of salvation. As Calvin comments:

> By meditating on that renovation which is laid up as the object of our hope, we may, with tranquil minds, suffer this frail tabernacle to be dissolved. There is, therefore, no reason why a feeble, emaciated body, failing eyes, tremulous hands, and the lost use of all our senses should so dishearten us, that we should not hasten, after the example of our father, with joy and alacrity to our death.[27]

This might well sound ridiculous at first glance: if we are nothing but an emaciated hulk, we might very well pursue death, let alone not be disheartened when it arrives. It is Calvin's strenuously religioethical connotation of fulfillment, however, that makes sense of this. Old age is a type of suffering in Calvin's perspective—a suffering justly inflicted on humans for their sins. Yet it is also a means of potentially strengthening the believer's trust and hope in God and the life to come by encouraging the turning of our thoughts to that eternal salvation. As Calvin writes, "the chief part of a good old age consists in a good conscience and in a serene and tranquil mind."[28] It is only those who "truly cultivate righteousness," however, who can attain this state and, as he suggests, "it is godliness which causes a good old age to attend us even to the grave, because faith is the preserver of a tranquil mind."[29] A good old age in Calvin's view, therefore, is that serenity of mind accompanying persistence in a life of righteous striving in the face of bodily dissolution.

AGING AS A PROCESS OF GROWTH

Many Witnesses in Tradition

A second claim that recurs frequently in certain aspects of the Christian theological tradition is that fulfillment in aging, as a blessing of God, is to be understood within the rubric of growth rather than decline. This can clearly be seen in Calvin's discussion, for example. Augustine took a similar position. At one point in his treatise *Of True Religion,* Augustine distinguished between "the exterior or earthly man" and "the heavenly or inward man." According to the former, human lives are marked by chronological years and the course of the body. Old age here, Augustine says, "is an inferior age, lacking in lustre, weak and more subject to disease."[30] According to the latter, however, "ages are marked, not according to years, but according to . . . spiritual advance."[31] Thus, in his sermon "To the Seekers of Baptism," Augustine writes: "In humility, seek; and when you have found, you will come to heights that are free from danger. Innocence will be your infancy; reverence, your childhood; patience, your adolescence; courage, your youth; merit, your manhood; and nothing other than venerable and wise discernment, your old age."[32] All these life divisions are not used chronologically, but spiritually, of course, but nonetheless the point is clear. The valuation of life is spiritual, not material and so, even in the chronological period of old age, life is to be marked by spiritual advance. As Ambrose wrote:

> What truly is old age if it is not a spotless life which is measured not by days or months, but by ages whose durability knows no end, whose longevity knows no weakness? The older it is, the stronger it is, and the longer he has lived that life, the more vigorously does he grow into the perfect man.[33]

As with Calvin, Augustine, and Ambrose, so with many other theological interpretations of old age, the Christian life is one of advance, progress, or growth. Old age, therefore, is to be marked by a similar process. The precise nature of this process, and the terms used to describe it, and the articulation of its goals or ends have varied considerably, as one might expect. Yet, there is often an underlying consistency to the structure of the argument.

The discussion of this process is usually premised in this way: chronological old age brings with it a dreaded physical decline—the powers of the body wane, the pursuits of young and middle adulthood become increasingly difficult if not impossible. As Jerome wrote, "All acts . . . of which the body is the medium decrease with its decay."[34] This association of chronological aging with, often horrifically portrayed, physical decline becomes a powerful image in many theological analyses. Friedrich Schleiermacher, for example, wrote in the final essay of his *Soliloquies:* "I will not see the dread infirmities of old age; I vow a mighty scorn of all adversity that does not touch that aim of my existence, and I pledge myself to an eternal Youth."[35] While Schleiermacher is using both "youth" and "old age" as broader metaphors in this context, it is yet revealing that he chose *those* terms. Nonetheless, the general structure of a variety of theological arguments concerning old age is premised by underscoring the association of the physical aspects of old age with bodily decline.

While the body declines and strength wanes, the theological tradition has generally understood human fulfillment in old age as in contradistinction to the course of physicality with aging. The most frequently cited distinction is that between body and spirit (or soul). Thus, while the body suffers deterioration with aging, the spirit or soul may yet grow in old age. In some cases, bodily decline in aging was positively valued since it was thought to free the aged from those things (usually the passions) which inhibit the workings of the spirit. As Jerome put it in a letter to Nepotian in 394:

> Youth, as such, has to cope with the assaults of passion, and amid the allurements of vice and the tinglings of the flesh is stifled like a fire among green boughs, and cannot develop its proper brightness. But when men have employed their youth in commendable pursuits and have meditated on the law of the Lord day and night, they learn with the lapse of time, fresh experience and wisdom come as the years go by, and so from the pursuits of the past their old age reaps a harvest of delight.[36]

Thus, many have argued that growth in old age is possible because those things most conducive to (or representative of) growth in the Christian life do not necessarily decline, but actually may increase with age. As the theologian Theodore Parker, for example, wrote:

[The older person's] affections now are greater than before; yet it is not the mere power of instinctive affection—the connubial instinct which loves a mate, or a parental instinct which loves a child; but a general human, reflective, volitional love, not sharpened by animal desire, nor narrowed by affiliated bounds, but coming of his freedom, not his bondage.[37]

Exactly what it is that is said to grow in old age varies considerably: piety, wisdom, spirit, moral acuity, and grace being only a few of the more frequently mentioned. That something intrinsic to the Christian life continues to grow despite bodily decline with aging, however, has been almost universally affirmed in the Christian theological tradition. In order to illustrate this claim, I will turn briefly to remarks of Chrysostom.

John Chrysostom

John Chrysostom sees human life as requiring continuing advance in the strengthening of the soul. In the homily on Heb. 4:11–13, he likens the Christian life to a race. Like a runner, Chrysostom says, the Christian has her goal only in view and pursues that goal with no attention to distractions. It is the prize that matters in a race, and so for the Christian life. It is not enough, however, that the race was run well at the beginning, there must be straining especially toward the end. As Chrysostom writes to those who leave discipline behind with youth: *"Now* most of all it behooves you to make your carefulness more intense. Do not count up to me the old things especially well done: be now youthful and vigorous."[38] As we saw with Calvin, the Christian life is not marked by rest or relief from the demands of that life in old age, but rather requires continued progress, continued advance.

Chrysostom is well aware, of course, that the body declines with aging and yet, he says, such decline does not detract from the central point: fulfillment in aging is to be understood within the rubric of progress of the soul rather than that of decline or decay of the body. Chrysostom remarks:

> For he that runneth this bodily race, when grey hairs have overtaken
> him, probably is not able to run as he did before; for the whole contest
> depends on the body; but thou—wherefore dost thou lessen thy speed?
> For in this race there is need of a soul, a soul thoroughly awakened: and
> the soul is rather strengthened in old age; then it is in its full vigor, then
> it is in its pride.[39]

Chrysostom's point is that fulfillment (at any age) is not a matter of
one's physical being, but rather that of the soul. As he writes at
several points, the beauty which the Christian seeks is not that of our
physical nature, which perishes with age, but rather the beauty of the
soul. Those who fail to cultivate the soul throughout life reap nothing but a harvest of grief.

Chrysostom believes that while fulfillment at any age is marked by
this orientation, the aged are at a special advantage. As with Jerome,
Chrysostom believes that the possibility of this spiritual advance
increases with age. Indeed, those things which most inhibit the soul
in earlier years ease their fervor with aging—freeing the older adult
somewhat for a more proper ordering of life. Chrysostom writes:

> For as the body, so long as it is oppressed by fevers and by one sickness
> after another, even if it be strong, is exhausted, but when it is freed
> from this attack, it recovers its proper force, so also the soul in youth is
> feverish, and is chiefly possessed by the love of glory, and luxurious
> living and sensual lusts, and many other imaginations; but old age,
> when it comes on, drives away all these passions, some through satiety,
> some through philosophy. For old age relaxes the powers of the body,
> and does not permit the soul to make use of them even if it wish, but
> representing them as enemies of various kinds, it sets here a place free
> from troubles and produces a great calm, and brings in greater fear.
> For if none else does, it is said, yet they who are grown old know that
> they are drawing to their end, and that they certainly stand near to
> death. When therefore the desires of this life are withdrawing, and the
> expectation of the judgment seat is coming on, softening the stubborn-
> ness of the soul, does it not become more attentive if one be willing?[40]

Thus, the growth or advance of the soul that is to mark old age,
Chrysostom says, is usually enabled by the course of our physical
nature with aging. Indeed, from Chrysostom's perspective we probably ought to celebrate this decline for it offers even greater possibility of turning rightly to God.

This greater possibility, of course, carries with it a greater burden
as well. What is expected of the aged greatly increases. In his homily

on John 9:17–35, Chrysostom writes: "I am especially ashamed . . . when I see a man, respected for his grey hairs, bringing shame on them, and dragging his son down with him. What indeed is more ridiculous than this? What deed more disgraceful."[41] While it is not clear if Chrysostom would have thought the deed was quite so disgraceful if it had involved the old man's daughter, the basic point is clear enough. What he sees as particularly grotesque in this is older adults committing the sins of the young. As he says, "For the hoary head is then venerable, when it acts worthily of the grey head; but when it plays youth, it will be more ridiculous than the young. How then will you old men be able to give these exhortations to the young men when you are intoxicated with your disorderliness?"[42]

Chrysostom was certainly not alone in taking this position. In the words of William Bridge some twelve centuries later, "there is a special repugnancy betwixt old men and youthful sins."[43] Or, as Mather put it in his usual style: "Nothing is more nauseous and odious in an old man than the levity of lasciviousness. For old men to talk bawdily and filthily and for old men to discover that the cursed fires of their youth are not yet extinguished in them, out with it."[44] Whatever else one might make of this, the general idea here is that old age is a special honor—a special blessing of God—and therefore the aged ought not to bring disgrace upon their years.

We might well wonder here what "youthful sins" Chrysostom had in mind that merited such vehement abhorence in old age. He writes:

> For the old man is a king, if you will, and more royal than he who wears the purple, if he master his passions, and keep them under subjection, in the ranks of the guards. But if he be dragged about and thrust down from his throne, and become a slave to the love of money, and vainglory, and personal adornment, and luxuriousness, and drunkenness, anger, and sensual pleasures, and has his hair dressed out with oil, and shows an age insulted by his way of life, of what punishment would not such an one be worthy?[45]

Thus, while the souls of the aged are to evidence youthful vigor, this is clearly to be differentiated from the youthful vigor of the passions. Those older adults who remain entangled in the follies of youth are subject to the most severe condemnation. Fulfillment in old age, therefore, rests upon the proper subjection of the passions with aging so that the soul might be freed to turn more fully and vigorously to higher things. Fulfillment in aging is to be a time of growth, progress, or advance—not of the body or the flesh or the passions, but of the soul.

THE RELIGIOETHICAL WITNESS OF AGE

As I have noted, many Christian theologians have understood old age as a blessing of God marked by continued growth or advance. Yet, as can be seen from the examples of Calvin and Chrysostom already discussed, this growth was understood in a particular religioethical form. Indeed, what I will call the religioethical witness of age was frequently seen as the manifestation of the blessing of age. Thus, as Ambrose wrote: "old age is truly venerable when it grows hoary not with grey hairs, but with good deeds. This hoariness is revered, hoariness of soul, gleaming with shining thoughts and deeds."[46]

To say that there is a religioethical witness of aging may well be the most peculiar-sounding aspect today of the interpretation of old age in the theological tradition. Indeed, we may well be tempted to see these discussions as quaintly antiquarian museum pieces. The ethical discussion of aging in our time certainly tends to have a different focus. Most of the contemporary ethical literature on aging has as its focus not the ethics of aging, but rather the ethics of caring for the aging; for example, what the social requirements of justice are with respect to the aged. We are met, in other words, with protracted arguments either defending or criticizing the variety of government-sponsored retirement and relief programs geared toward the aged. This is, of course, an important issue, but it leaves open the question of the moral praxis of aging itself. Likewise, there is extraordinarily little discussion in the theological literature on the ethics of aging. Thus, when the seventeenth-century English Puritan theologian Richard Baxter cites fifteen duties of the aged in his *Christian Directory*, we are apt to be taken aback. As I will later suggest, however, what we are likely to be taken aback by is not so much Baxter's moral concern as by his audacious honesty about it.

When a culture hides its morality under the guise of "feelings," though, we might well expect some sense of disjunction with the historic theological tradition on this point.

Meditation

Precisely what the religioethical witness of age was thought to consist of varied a great deal. Yet, its principal focus was establishing or maintaining a right relation to God. In practical terms this meant two things. First, meditation (in the form of both repentance and reminiscence) was of special importance for the aged. Since the aged were nearing their end, it was thought to be of critical importance for them to meditate on the course of their lives and the glory of God so as to place their souls rightly before the Almighty. Bridge, for example, speaks of the aged looking forward to the "glorious mansions and inheritance lying in the field of eternity":

> What, then, though your turf house now be ready to fire into a fever with every spark of distemper, is there not enough in that house above to pay for all? Surely there is. Why then should ye not lift up your heads, ye old men, and be of good comfort under all your natural infirmities.[47]

Calvin, Mather, Ambrose, and, as we shall see, Baxter make related points.

Teaching the Young

Second, however, establishing or maintaining a right relation to God in old age also meant carrying out the moral responsibilities incumbent upon the aged. Principal among these was that of instructing the younger generations. Appropriate meditation was, of course, one means of doing so, yet there were others as well. According to Clement of Alexandria, for example, even the mere presence of the aged served this purpose in relation to more raucous youth: "And above all, old age, which conciliates trust, is not to be concealed. But God's mark of honor [gray hair] is to be shown in the light of day, to win the reverence of the young. For sometimes, when they have been behaving shamefully the appearance of hoary hairs, arriving like an instructor, has changed them to sobriety and paralyzed juvenile lust with the splendor of the sight."[48] Whatever form it was thought best to take, the Christian theological tradition has frequently contended that it is a primary duty of the aged to teach the young and to impart the wisdom of their years to those less furnished in long experience. As Mather wrote:

> Husband well every minute of the little time that is left, by always being employed for the good of them that shall come after you. . . . You must be found in faith. You are our teachers, our tutors; our eyes are upon you for a tradition of the faith once delivered unto the saints.[49]

The usual basis for this claim was that the many years the older individual had lived potentially provided much instructive material on the nature and benefit of right living. While it was clearly noted that not all older persons had profited by their long experience, those who had were thought to have a duty to impart it. The corresponding obligation of the younger generations, of course, was to pay attention to this witness of age.

In certain important aspects of the historic Christian theological tradition, therefore, human fulfillment in old age was not simply a matter of self-actualization or "doing your own thing." There were quite clear expectations of older adults. Indeed, fulfillment in old age in most cases was seen as bound to the older adult's contributing to the potential fulfillment of the younger generations. Yet, as I have noted, the obligations between the generations were understood as mutual. In other words, the interpretation of human fulfillment with aging found throughout much of the historic Christian theological tradition hinged on an understanding of community and social interchange which underscored the moral and religious interconnection of the generations.

Duties of the Aged

In chapter 29 of the *Christian Directory,* entitled "Directions for the Aged and Weak," Baxter cites fifteen duties of the aged. One is immediately struck both by the similarities and the subtle differences in relation to Calvin's view of fulfillment in old age. Baxter, for example, often treats aging as if it is a type of suffering, but he does not suggest that old age is caused by sin.

Every aged person, whether "regenerate and sanctified or not" Baxter contends, must carefully examine "the state of their souls" to determine as best they can "how all things stand between God" and themselves.[50] This is especially important for the aged, Baxter writes, because they are so near their end. The aged must continually keep their sins in view so as to motivate them to turn rightly to God:

> Though you have repented and been justified long ago, yet you have daily sinned since you were justified; and though all be forgiven that is repented of, yet must it be still before your eyes, both to keep you humble, and continue the exercise of that repentance, and drive you to Christ, and make you thankful.[51]

We must not only keep our sins in view, however, but also must meditate on God's mercies toward us: "This is the great privilege of an aged Christian, that he hath many years mercy more to think on, than others have."[52] In a passage similar to some contemporary psychological perspectives on reminiscence in old age (which, of course, do not contain Baxter's explicitly religious context), Baxter writes:

> What delightful work it is for your thoughts, to look back to your childhood, and remember how mercy brought you up and conducted you to every place you have lived in; and provided for you, and preserved you, and heard your prayers, and disposed of all things for your good. . . . And is it not a pleasant work in old age to ruminate upon them? If a traveller delight to talk of his travels, and a soldier or seaman, upon his adventures, how sweet should it be to a Christian to peruse all the conduct of mercy through his life and all the operations of Spirit upon his heart.[53]

Such reminiscence, though, is not simply a "pleasant work" in Baxter's view. Rather, it is also a means of overcoming the inevitable decline in aging. As Baxter writes concerning reminiscence on God's mercies toward us: "such thankful reviews of ancient mercies will force an ingenuous soul to a quieter submission to infirmities, sufferings, and death."[54] In a passage that underscores the necessity of turning to the "spiritual," Baxter argues:

> Take not a decay of nature, and of those gifts and works which depend thereon, for a decay of grace. Though your memory, and utterance, and fervour of affection, abate as your natural heat abateth, yet be not discouraged; but remember, that for all this you may grow in grace. If you do but grow in holy wisdom and judgment, and a higher esteem of God and holiness, and a greater disesteem of all the vanities of the world, and a firmer resolution to cleave to God and trust in Christ, and never to turn to the world and sin; this is your growth in grace.[55]

Though the body declines with aging, older adults have a special responsibility in Baxter's view: the aged must teach the younger and less wise. Indeed, "God hath made this the duty of the aged, that the 'Fathers should tell the wonders of his works and mercies to their children, that the ages to come may praise the Lord.'"[56] The aged are to teach not only through the direct imparting of information, but also by being living "examples of wisdom, gravity, and holiness unto the younger."[57]

This duty on the part of the aged is accompanied by a corresponding duty on the part of the younger members of society. In his *Compassionate Counsel to Young Men,* Baxter writes that:

> Nature and Scripture tell us that the younger owe much duty to the elder, which is thus summed up, "Ye, Younger, submit yourselves to the Elder." (1 Peter v. 5). This submission includeth, especially a reverence to their judgments, preferring them before their own; and a reasonable supposition that ordinarily the elder are wiser than they, and therefore living towards their elders in a humble and learning disposition, not proudly setting their own unfurnished wits against the greater experience of their elders, without very evident and extraordinary reasons.[58]

Baxter does not suggest that great age alone is sufficient to ensure wisdom. Indeed, he says without qualification that "none are more sottishly and incurably ignorant than those who are both aged and ignorant, and few are so bad as old and obstinate sinners."[59] God may, in fact, bless some young persons with greater understanding and wisdom than some older persons. However, by far the more natural course of events, Baxter believes, is for the aged to be wiser since "long experience is far more powerful than that which is short" and "young men cannot be ripe in wisdom without a miracle."[60] Baxter is reiterating a commonly held ideal of seventeenth-century England. In speaking of age relations in that period, the historian Keith Thomas has noted that "Knowledge was supposed to flow down from old to young, with cultural and ideological predominance remaining firmly in the hands of the elderly. Youth was notoriously unfit to teach youth."[61] As Thomas indicates, such an ideal served as justification for maintaining the economic status of the middle- and old-aged through its implementation in legal statutes; for example, those prescribing extraordinarily lengthy apprenticeship periods.[62] Whatever its ideological underpinnings, the aged in Baxter's view had a primary duty to teach the young and to impart the wisdom of their years to those less furnished in long experience.

The understanding of human fulfillment with aging for Baxter centers around the question of how one is to deal with the decline and losses associated with aging. His practical theology principally takes the form of various prescriptions or directions to cope with such decline and loss. These prescriptions are truly religioethical duties; that is, duties which are grounded in an explicitly religious context and which have moral import. Thus, for example, even though Baxter allows that one is permitted to "disengage" somewhat from active participation in society, as one's physical condition warrants, Baxter suggests that even this "disengagement" serves not just God alone, but other humans as well. Therefore, the reminiscence of the aged, while on the one hand encouraging appropriate coping with the individual's own decline, is yet, on the other hand, a means of instructing the "inexperienced and ungodly."

Fulfillment in old age for Baxter involves establishing the right relationship on the part of the aged toward God. This is no simple individualistic doctrine, however, but rather suggests the interconnection of one's own fulfillment with facilitating the fulfillment of others. As Baxter writes in his final direction to the aged:

Let all the high and glorious things, which faith apprehendeth, now show their power in the love, and joy, and longings of your soul. . . . This will do much to convince unbelievers, that the promises are true, and that heaven is real, and that a holy life is indeed the best, which hath so happy an end. When they see you highest in your joys, at the time when others are deepest in distress; and when you rejoice as one that is entering upon his happiness when all the happiness of the ungodly is at an end; this will do more than many sermons, to persuade a sinner to holy life. I know that this is not easily attained; but a thing so sweet and profitable to yourselves, and so useful to the good of others, and so much tending to the honor of God should be labored after with all your diligence: and then you may expect God's blessing on your labors.[63]

TOWARD A CONTEMPORARY UNDERSTANDING OF HUMAN FULFILLMENT IN OLD AGE

To have offered an interpretation of how certain aspects of the Christian theological tradition have historically tended to understand human fulfillment with aging is not to have offered an interpretation that easily, or even necessarily, fits with contemporary knowledge and experience. Our understanding of human fulfillment in old age in the latter half of the twentieth century cannot simply be the reiteration of interpretations offered in the fourth, sixteenth, or eighteenth century. Yet, to the extent we wish to understand ourselves within the Christian tradition, we cannot simply jettison the history of Christian discourse on aging because it was written in sociohistorical contexts that are not our own or simply because (the ultimate caveat of the age of satisfaction) it does not "feel right."

Our task, rather, is to think through the historic claims critically from within the context of contemporary views of aging and in light of the contemporary arguments of the theological subdisciplines. This is, of course, an exceedingly complex task and I do not pretend in what follows to have answered (or even addressed) all of the difficult issues. I am guided by the more modest hope that at least the outlines of a coherent position will be made apparent. Such at least seems essential if those engaged in pastoral care with older adults are to have a sense of what it means to re-present the church's mission and witness in our time.

CHAPTER 4

Of Nature and Spirit

> There is no state or condition of men, but some grace, goodness, or
> virtue may and can plant upon; . . . It is our wisdom, therefore, to
> observe what our state and soil is, and to plant our ground accordingly.[1]

What, to use William Bridge's words, is the "state and soil" of old
age? For Bridge, old age was a "dry and barren ground."[2] Yet,
Bridge thought—as did much of the theological tradition in
general—that growth was still possible in this dry and barren
ground. Indeed, *fulfillment* in aging was generally seen as marked by
growth. As we will see, the idea of "growth" in this context had
particular meanings that are likely to seem tied to distant cultures
today. The question, however, remains a haunting one: Is old age
simply a matter of increasing and increasingly intense loss or, within
this context, can we still speak meaningfully of growth?

The peculiarity for us today of the claim that fulfillment in aging is
marked by growth lies in two directions. First, it may seem trite or
simply obvious that *fulfillment* at whatever stage of life is a matter of
growth and not decline. The piety of self-actualization in our time is
such that "growth" appears the sine qua non of the most desirable
way of life. Yet, I suspect that when we wonder what we could really
mean by "growth," the flippancy of the appeal to "actualization" in
this regard is rendered less apparent. In some respects, of course, we
have already learned that lesson. However fully we may have
granted the difficulty of making adequate sense of the idea of
growth with respect to most life periods, though, aging is still seriously susceptible to the sentimentalizing and romanticizing of
"growth."

Perhaps this is a reaction to the second peculiarity of the idea of growth with aging: aging and *decline* seem such a natural pair. Some of the most powerful images of aging attest to this association: the aged Nestor of Homer's *Iliad,* the exiled Oedipus of Sophocles' *Oedipus Colunus,* the pathetic older persons of Juvenal's *Satires,* the grim portrayal of the "evil days" in Ecclesiastes, the ridiculous Lady Wishfort of William Congreves's *The Way of the World,* and the decaying Krapp of Samuel Beckett's *Krapp's Last Tape.* The association of aging with decline and loss in our experience is frequently so powerful that we seem to be left with either simply rejecting the idea of growth with aging altogether or romanticizing it to avoid the seemingly too painful realities.

Our sense of what "growth" and "loss" mean with respect to aging, of course, is relative to a number of things: some having to do with the broader range of theoretical constructs within which those ideas are set for us, some having to do with personal and sociohistorical dynamics unique to us, our cultural location, or our time. Our focus in this chapter is on one aspect of all this: the understanding of human nature and human development with aging which under-girds and makes foundational sense of what we could mean by "growth" in aging. Before addressing this directly, however, it may prove helpful to clarify how this issue confronts us in pastoral care with the aging.

PASTORAL CARE AND THE
QUESTION OF GROWTH

Is pastoral care with older adults principally a matter of facilitating growth or of enabling appropriate coping with loss and decline? While this question is, of course, outrageously simplistic and unanswerable in the abstract, the issues it raises impinge directly on an aspect of that interpretive lens through which those engaged in pastoral care with older adults "see" the issues and concerns they face. A brief case study may help us sharpen the issues somewhat.

The Case of Margaret Arnold

Margaret Arnold was a 72-year-old woman who had been a widow for some ten years. She lived by herself in the home in which she and her husband had raised their sole child, a son now married and living in the same city. She went to see a pastoral counselor upon the recommendation of her minister. Of timid appearance, she was concerned about "bad thoughts" she had been experiencing: fantasies having to do with sexual intercourse and with causing physical harm to herself and others. While these particular fantasies began some three years after the death of her husband, they had become intensified in the previous year—a year marked by increasing physical ailments and illnesses. She was frightened by her fantasies and felt she was morally wrong to have them, but found no way to stop them from occupying increasing amounts of her time.

Margaret Arnold was the eldest of three children: she had a brother two years younger and a sister five years younger than herself. Her parents had immigrated to this country from Norway at the turn of the century. Her father was a binge alcoholic and held sporadic employment as a sales clerk. Margaret described him as frightening and angry when drunk, but "very nice and kind" when sober. Her mother worked part time as a nurse to support the family and was experienced by Margaret as frequently indifferent in the face of the family turmoil. But, then, Margaret said, her mother had "taken a lot" during the marriage, "more than I would have." When Margaret was twenty, her parents arranged a marriage for her with the son of a friend of her father. Her husband also drank heavily and the marriage, like her childhood, lacked warmth and affection.

Clearly, the unresolved Oedipal dimensions of her relation to her father continued to mark her experience. But, more generally, Margaret's life unfolded and was shaped in the context of unreliable others. She adapted to this warm/cold, present/absent climate by withdrawing into an elaborate romantic fantasy world when she was young and by evolving a passive style in relation to others which, yet, barely concealed the rage and terror which lay beneath it. While she was not particularly pleased with her usual ways of dealing with conflict, she had felt relatively comfortable within them. At present, however, the previously comfortable, now-crumbling defenses seemed on the verge of collapse.

Growth or Decline?

Is the task of the pastoral counselor here to enable Margaret Arnold's growth or to enable her to cope more appropriately with loss and decline? To put it another (and better) way, are Margaret

Arnold's intensified concerns about her "bad thoughts" to be seen within a developmental psychology of aging, as regressive phenomena (or disintegration products) in the face of inevitable and irreversible loss, or as basically untransformed dynamics of her childhood development? My point in raising these questions is to note that answers to them are theory-specific. In other words, what (if anything) counts as "growth" with aging or what counts as "loss" with aging is dependent, at least in part, upon the theoretical constructs through which those ideas are being interpreted.

The predominant orientation would tend to see Margaret Arnold's intensified concerns as the product of past maladaptation exacerbated by current losses. As the psychologist David Gutmann has written: "By and large, the geropsychiatrist looks on his elderly patients as metaphors of irretrievable decline; as a consequence, the symptoms of the older patient are almost invariably referred to as current losses in the somatic, social, cognitive, or existential domain."[3] The therapeutic task from such a perspective is to help older individuals cope with those losses and declining abilities (and, thus, to put a roadblock in the way of the regression) so as to stabilize the level of functioning.

There is a growing body of literature, however, suggesting alternative formulations (as we shall see in the following chapter). Gutmann's own recent theoretical formulations suggest, for example, the importance of wondering whether Mrs. Arnold's symptoms are not merely the reemergence and intensification of past problems, but a reemergence of them in restated form, that is, in the context of particular psychological developments that emerge with aging. These suggestions notwithstanding, actual practice is still often tied to the "aging as loss" paradigm.

In order to interpret both what is going on and what ought to be done in this situation, Mrs. Arnold's pastoral counselor will, at least implicitly, have some understanding of what "loss" and "growth" mean as these relate to older adults. It is precisely certain aspects of this issue that this chapter seeks to address. To take the Christian theological tradition seriously in its claim that fulfillment in aging embodies growth requires that we seek to determine whether (and, if so, how) the idea of growth in aging can make sense today. To begin to work through this issue, we must first return to the theological tradition.

DUALISM IN THE TRADITION

Bodily Decay, Spiritual Growth

Given the biological realities of growing older, how is it that the Christian tradition could claim that growth is possible in old age? Those aspects of the theological tradition with which we are concerned here, of course, had a particular understanding of human nature that made sense of the idea of growth for the aging. The question we must face in this chapter is whether this understanding is viable today.

The rejection of the "aging as loss" paradigm as forming the normative context for understanding aging often rested upon a distinction between the symbolism of permanence and transience, the "eternal things" and the "things which shall pass away." This frequently involved understanding human nature as composed of two elements or qualities: one more characterized by finitude and transience, the other more characterized by permanence and its potential for participation (if only through the activity of knowing or intuition) in the divine. In many instances, this meant the valuative association of the soul or spirit with the pole of permanence and the body or nature with the pole of transience. Thus, while the physical body decays with aging, the soul or spirit may yet grow. Nature is subject to the cycle of growth and decay (thus, the decline of our physical being with aging), while spirit (when rightly related to God) may continually "advance in newness of life."

Thus, this distinction between nature and spirit often resulted in spirit being associated with permanence, the "high" in humans, and the truly valuable or worthy, while nature was associated with transience, the "low," and the corrupting. Spirit was the locus of mind, reason, will, or faith and was, therefore, the avenue to the good (and God). Nature (or the body) was the ever-present seducer or, in less gross terms, that which required proper ordering by the spirit. To put this another way, there is a *tendency* toward a dualistic anthropology in much of the historic Christian theological literature on aging.

The distinctions I have suggested here are somewhat overdrawn. As David Kelsey has observed, even most classic theological anthropologies do not seem to have intended such gross devaluations of the natural or physical. Yet, as Kelsey notes, "it must be acknowledged that the body/soul conceptual schema employed in classic formulations permitted and probably encouraged such attitudes."[4] Certainly, this tendency is evidenced in discussions of aging. The allurements of the flesh, the fire of the passions, and the lusts of the body are set in stringent contradistinction to spiritual advance, piety, and the proper alignment of the soul with aging.

We can see this quite clearly in the cases of Jerome and John Chrysostom, for example. It is as the passions subside with aging that the activity of the soul may reach full flower. Fulfillment in aging entailed the proper subjecting or ordering of the body (or nature) by the spirit (or soul). While this dualistic tendency is less pronounced in the discussions of old age by, for example, John Calvin, Richard Baxter, and Theodore Parker, there is yet a relatively clear dichotomy drawn between nature and spirit that tends in a similar direction. Likewise, Friedrich Schleiermacher wrote that: "The decline of vigor and strength is an ill that man inflicts upon himself; old age is but an idle prejudice, an ugly fruit of the mad delusion that the spirit is dependent upon the body."[5] We must be cautious in this, of course, for there is great subtlety in what Schleiermacher means in its broader context, yet the imagery is striking. Again, however, my point in this is not to claim that any of these theologians were simple dualists, but rather that there is a significant dualistic tendency that arises in their discussions of aging.

Moving Beyond Dualism

One of the hallmarks of postmodern thought, however, is precisely the rejection of such dualistic tendencies—whether in Platonic or Cartesian forms. What does this mean for our understanding of growth in aging? It means that such dualistic tendencies as undergirded much of the historic theological understanding of growth in aging can no longer be seen adequately to sustain the idea. As the philosopher Mary Midgley has succinctly put the hard premise of our time with respect to this: "We are not just rather like animals; we are animals."[6] While Midgley certainly does not mean to deny that there are significant differences between humans and other animals, she does wish to point out by this that our higher capacities (speech, rationality, and culture) are not distinct from nature but rather special developments within it.

The works of Midgley, Konrad Lorenz, George Pugh, Donald Campbell, and Victor Turner on the significance of adaptive-evolutionary analyses for understanding our "higher" capacities, the works of Sigmund Freud, Carl Jung, Erik Erikson, and Heinz Kohut on the archaic and primitive dimensions of much of what we count as "maturity," and the works of Karl Marx, Max Weber, and Jurgen Habermas on the intricate relation between the material contexts of our lives and our highest spiritual achievements have all rendered dualistic notions dubious at best. Such is the case in much of contemporary theology as well. The rejection of "super-naturalism" and nonpraxis epistemologies in liberation theology and the organic and social vision of reality in process theology are but two examples. The theologian Schubert Ogden has well stated the general point I want to make of all this:

> There is every reason to believe that human existence has emerged from nature and is itself entirely natural. Its most distinctive characteristics, such as the capacity for true speech and self-consciousness, realize some of nature's own potentialities, instead of in any way distinguishing it as non-natural.[7]

The tendency toward dualism that we found in much of the historic theological understanding of aging tended to interpret human nature as composed of two elements or qualities: one natural, one nonnatural (spirit, soul, etc.). While this latter quality may have been seen as inevitably immersed in the processes of nature in its concrete embodiment in human being, there was yet something essentially nonnatural about it. The point I am making, however, in line with the comments of Ogden and Midgley, is that the "high" in humans (whether we call it spirit, soul, or something else) is entirely natural and historical.[8]

The nondualistic interpretation of human being, while receiving ample support from the physical and human sciences, has been hard to swallow for some. The traditional dualism of human beings as composed of nature and spirit is well entrenched in our cultural history. Yet, in terms of the Christian witness, there seems every theological and even scriptural reason to reject it. Indeed, it has by now long been convincingly argued that even the biblical sources do not support such an interpretation. The German Old Testament scholar Claus Westermann has noted that the Genesis account of creation maintains that human being is created as a complete unity. A division of human being into body and soul, or body, soul, and spirit, is not justified by the texts. All that belongs to human existence is included. "It [the Bible] does not allow for any division, anthropologically speaking, into flesh and spirit, even less for an undervaluing of the flesh and an overvaluing of the spirit."[9] Thus, the tendency toward dualism which was often utilized to make sense of the idea of growth with aging in the theological tradition no longer seems justified: we do not merely contain a natural component, even our "higher" capacities must be seen as developments within nature.

Dualistic tendencies do not generally permeate the contemporary pastoral care literature on aging, however. Given the influence of contemporary psychology on the practice of pastoral care, it is unlikely that many of those engaged in pastoral care with older adults would see, for example, Margaret Arnold's "bad thoughts" simply as seducing or corrupting her soul or the more spiritual dimensions of her life. We would be hard pressed, I suspect, to find many who would think the task here is simply to "convict" Mrs. Arnold of her inordinate love of self so as to free her soul from those "bad thoughts" for higher matters.

While dualism is not the substantive problem in the contemporary literature, yet it often forms the contextual problem. That is, much of the literature still sees dualism as the principal position to be overcome. There is, of course, at least a degree of justification for this. In certain aspects of popular culture, the passions are still seen as out of place or inappropriate in older adults. The symbolism of the "dirty old man" and the "old hag" reveal not only the gender differentiation of stereotypes of aging, but also a general disparagement of the passions in older adults.[10] Indeed, some older adults themselves come to the minister or pastoral counselor with dualistic interpretations of their concerns, which mirror this broader cultural orientation. Mrs. Arnold's guilt about her "bad thoughts," for example, was often expressed in just such a fashion: sex was "dirty, especially for someone of my age."

This sort of thing is obviously important when it arises in pastoral care. Yet, if the dualistic tendencies of the historic theological understanding of aging can no longer be maintained, what understanding of human nature and human development is relatively more adequate? If we think, for example, that dualistic understandings of the elderly's concerns and hopes are mistaken with respect to how human beings actually function, within what understanding of human nature with aging is the agent of pastoral care to ground her diagnoses and interventions? If we can no longer appeal to non-natural components of human being that advance or grow despite the decline of our natural elements, must we reject the notion of growth with aging altogether as simple wishful thinking? We have often tended in this latter direction. We can see this quite clearly in the modern biological and human science literature, where the "aging as loss" paradigm has historically held powerful sway.

CULTURAL ROOTS OF THE "AGING AS LOSS" PARADIGM

The "aging as loss" paradigm, of course, has a history which far precedes the development of the modern human sciences. For example, in the *Rhetoric* Aristotle noted that the course of life after middle adulthood was downward in most important respects. Yet, given the pervasive influence of the human sciences on our self-understanding today, it may prove useful to sketch briefly some of the contemporary vicissitudes of the "aging as loss" paradigm in that literature.

In the early part of this century, for example, the influential Parisian bacteriologist Elie Metchnikoff argued that aging was pathological per se.[11] As the historian Andrew Achenbaum has shown, Metchnikoff was certainly not alone in this estimation. The idea that old age simply *is* pathogenic had wide-ranging currency. However quickly the biological underpinnings of Metchnikoff's own theory eroded, the general theme persisted that old age was simply a matter of progressive deterioration.

A more recent example from the biological literature that suggests the entrenched character of the problem is found in the work of the late biogerontologist George Sacher. Sacher sought to shift the biological concern with aging from a vision of a potentially perfect organism trapped by inevitable, random processes of decline and death, to a vision of an inherently finite organism that may, nonetheless, extend (Sacher said "transcend") its finitude through the orderly processes of evolution or through genetic manipulation. Thus, the underlying thrust of Sacher's interpretation rested upon the hope of "transcending" the processes of decline:

> Gerontology is not the science of aging, for that definition is a concession of defeat. It should be considered to be the science of life in the aspect of its finitude, because this more general definition puts aging in proper perspective with longevity and death, and points to the possibility of an evolutionarily and humanistically meaningful transcendence of finitude as a result of future biological research.[12]

Even Sacher's attempt to reformulate the issue, however, clearly echoes the "aging as loss/decline" paradigm. Why else would the idea of gerontology as the "science of aging" necessarily be seen as a *defeat?*

While interpretations of the biological realities of aging have frequently contributed to the "aging as loss" paradigm, such perspectives have found their way also into sociological and psychological understandings. In Morton Lieberman and Sheldon Tobin's recent study *The Experience of Old Age,* for example, the central psychological challenges facing the elderly are said to be "dealing with losses of various kinds, lessened control over their lives, and the absence of clearly defined roles."[13]

Undoubtedly the most influential gerontological theory of the past several decades, disengagement theology, embodied the "aging as loss" orientation.[14] In its original form, disengagement theory was based on two propositions: (1) with aging there is a mutual withdrawal between the individual and the society, and (2) this mutual withdrawal is good for the aged (that is, it leads to "successful" or "healthy" aging). As Erdman Palmore has noted about disengagement theory: " [Disengagement] is good for the aged because it is an acceptance of the inevitable decline and death, a conservation of energy as the best way to adapt to the declining abilities of old age."[15]

As I noted in the first chapter, this general perspective was the understanding of human nature in old age informing the responses of Rev. Williams to George and Betty Anderson. Old age was seen as a period of progressive loss and decline by Rev. Williams and the appropriate response to this was to facilitate the withdrawal of the Andersons from the broader society. While disengagement theory is rarely defended in its original form today, Rev. Williams's understanding was yet consistent with a more general cultural orientation that disengagement theory itself codified in a particular form: aging *is* loss.

Nonetheless, it is now beyond doubt that disengagement theory in its global form is not appropriate either as a description of what happens to the relationship between the aged and society or as an evaluative framework for facilitating adaptive or successful aging.[16] The issue is not resolved, however, simply by moving from disengagement theory to what is frequently seen as its opposite—often called "activity theory." Indeed, while activity theory remains a rather loosely formulated group of hypotheses (and may or may not be a true opposite of "disengagement"), it is yet frequently discussed within the context of the more general "aging as loss" perspective. What often changes in the move from disengagement to activity as the interpretive framework is not the overarching paradigm, but rather simply the way in which one is said most successfully to adapt to that progressive decline which *is* aging.

Another area in which the human science understanding of aging historically tended to be guided by the "aging as loss" perspective is the study of cognitive functioning. The late gerontological psychologist R. L. Kahn noted (in personal communication) a classic instance of this in the association of selective impairment of cognitive functioning in the brain-damaged with the course of cognitive functioning with aging. The idea here was that being old was like being brain-damaged. Likewise, much of the early life course literature on cognitive functioning seemed to suggest an ineluctable decline with aging on both verbal and problem-solving dimensions of intelligence.

Beginning in the early 1970s, however, it was becoming increasingly clear that the association of aging with inevitable cognitive decline was not appropriate.[17] Conflicts between cross-sectional and longitudinal studies of cognitive development led some to speak of the "myth of intellectual decline" with aging.[18] These disputes will no doubt continue for some time. Perhaps the most provocative outcome of all this, however, has been the proposal of alternative models where cognitive functioning in later adulthood is seen not as a simple extension of earlier processes (in relation to which it may evince decline), but rather as undergoing developmental changes affecting the orientation and function of certain of these processes.[19]

As I noted in the previous chapter, the understanding of aging found in much of the historic theological literature on aging certainly recognized the realities of loss and decline in aging. Indeed, strictly within the realm of "nature" and chronological age, aging was seen as principally a matter of decline. Yet these discussions generally rejected loss and decline as the *normative* context within which to understand growing older. As I have already observed, though, the underlying understanding of human nature that made sense of this no longer seems viable. I do not think this means we must accept the "aging as loss" paradigm. There are at least two alternative models of human functioning prominent today which allow for the possibility of growth with aging. There are rather severe differences between them and, thus, it will prove useful briefly to examine both.

UNDIALECTICAL PROGRESSIVISM

While the separation of nature and spirit is no longer accepted in such broad terms as the tendency toward dualism in the theological literature on aging implied, there is still a tendency to concentrate on the "high" in humans when discussing the nature of the good or of human fulfillment in aging. I will call this, following Don Browning, an undialectically progressive approach to understanding human development.[20] The undialectically progressive understanding, while not disparaging or explicitly separating out the "low" or nature, yet fails to appreciate the full interaction or dialectic involved in human development. In other words, human development is seen as simply a forward movement or progression from the immature to the mature. The understanding of growth in aging here is bought at the price of obscuring the inevitable archaic and primitive dimensions of personality. Two brief examples from the contemporary literature may help clarify the issues involved in this.

In their popularly written book, *Aging: The Fulfillment of Life*, Henri Nouwen and Walter Gaffney write:

The vision which grows in aging can lead us beyond the limitations of our human self. It is a vision that makes us not only detach ourselves from preoccupation with the past, but also from the importance of the present. It is a vision that invites us to a total, fearless surrender in which the distinction between life and death slowly loses its pain.[21]

While one might admire the stirring quality of the vision here, there is a sense in which the processes of decline and the inevitable limitations wrought by advancing years are not fully appreciated (either in their biological or their intrapsychic senses). They remark, for example, that "We believe that aging is not a reason for despair but a basis for hope, not a slow decaying but a gradual maturing, not a fate to be undergone but a chance to be embraced."[22] The problem here is that Nouwen and Gaffney tend to define away the harder polarities of the aging self: surely there is both despair and hope, decaying and maturing, fate undergone and a chance embraced. Given this defining away of the ambiguities, their interpretation subsequently tends to obscure the primitive realities and energies of the aging self. Fulfillment becomes identified with high level ego-integrative or synthetic functioning—if not in opposition to lower or more primitive functioning, then at least in spite of them. Thus, while Nouwen and Gaffney's image is certainly not dualistic in the classic sense, it is yet undialectically progressive.

William Clements's recent book *Care and Counseling of the Aging,* while distinctly helpful and instructive on many matters, also seems to lean in this direction at times. Much of his discussion of the developmental crises of old age, for example, deals primarily with these crises as simple conscious conflicts. Development here tends to take on the tone of overcoming and moving beyond the conflicts, rather than dynamically carrying forward and restating. This is suggested, for example, in his discussion of "body transcendence" with aging:

Persons who have chosen to transcend their bodily aches and pains experience no less discomfort than others, who worry unduly about their bodies, but their sense of well-being seems to rest on something other than physical comfort alone. If I, for example, base my sense of happiness on rewarding human relationships and creative mental activities, then physical discomfort is not experienced as a threat to "me", but more as a problem to be solved or an impediment to be skirted in the movement toward proximate goals.[23]

The problem with this type of discussion is that it rests almost entirely on the language of conscious volition. Whether Clements really means it this way, it tends to give the impression that "growth" is just a matter of good fortune and making the right conscious resolve. Yet, the inability of many to make such a resolve efficacious and the ambiguous ways in which others do make such resolves efficacious suggest that conscious volition is but a part of the issue. What is missing, in other words, is a sense of the dialectical interplay of the "higher" and "lower" functioning that is expressed in such volition. This omission tends to push some aspects of Clements's discussion in the direction of an undialectical progressivism.

Whereas interpretations with dualistic tendencies see growth with aging as a matter of wresting the progress of the spirit from the throes of the passions or of spiritual advance independent of the course of "nature," undialectically progressive interpretations see growth as the relatively unidirectional movement from the immature and archaic to the more mature and higher-level processes and functioning. While undialectically progressive interpretations permit a variety of permutations, an example of this approach might see the task of pastoral care with Mrs. Arnold as primarily one of enabling her to accept her "bad thoughts" in order to help her move beyond the present impasse and allow her to establish her life around a less truncated sense of self. The hallmark of the undialectically progressive interpretation of this situation would be its failure fully to recognize that the more primitive and archaic dimensions of personality are never *undialectically* transcended, moved beyond, or skirted. Sexuality and aggressiveness (the latter perhaps understood as "confrontiveness" or "assertiveness") would tend to be seen more in the context of their higher manifestations and relatively divorced or alienated from their archaic and primitive dimensions.

GROWTH AND DIALECTICAL
PROGRESSIVISM

The claim that fulfillment in aging entails continuing growth can no longer adequately be sustained either by dualistic or undialectically progressive interpretations of human beings. The perspective on development which I think is more adequate has already been implied in much of what I have said above: dialectical progressivism. Dialectical progressivism maintains that human development does not proceed simply toward "higher level" functioning, but rather always represents a progressive, yet dialectical interplay between "high" and "low." Thus, what we often think of as the "high" in humans (capacities for reason and morality, the "mature" or developmentally later) are neither divorced from nor simply subsume the "low" (the dynamics of instincts, the passions, fantasy, developmentally early needs and wishes). As the psychoanalyst Hans Loewald has put it:

> There is no one-way street from id to ego. Not only do irrational forces overtake us again and again; in trying to lose them we would be lost . . . individual development could be described as an ascending spiral in which the same basic themes are re-experienced and enacted on different levels of mentation and action.[24]

Thus, human development should be seen neither as a bare repetition of earlier dynamics or as, in Loewald's phrase, a straight-line progression from the immature to the mature, but rather as a progressive yet dialectical interplay between the high and low, the mature and the immature.

As this relates to aging, it suggests that aging ought to be understood developmentally neither as a purely regressive psychological phenomenon in the face of loss/decline nor a movement outside or simply beyond the more developmentally archaic, primitive dimensions of personality. Rather the dialectically progressive interpretation rests on two claims: (1) the "low" or developmentally early persists in later years, but (2) it persists in restated form, that is, in the context of the central developmental challenges of growing older.

We can illustrate this by suggesting how some of these issues might be seen in the case of Margaret Arnold. The dialectically progressive interpretation asks us to consider this possibility with regard to her situation: that it is not simply regressive, but contains regressive components in the face of an overarching developmental task. It asks us to see the probably narcissistic and, perhaps even hysteric, dynamics of her life not *simply* as unresolved dynamics of her childhood development, but as contextualized by and restated in the face of the central challenges she now confronts. Margaret Arnold brings to the central challenges of her latter years a troubled array of adaptive styles, distortions in her object-relations, and powerful, ego-dystonic fantasies. That these dynamics have deep roots in her childhood is not to be doubted. But dialectical progressivism asks us to consider these dynamics as not simply carried forward in static fashion, but as continually reformed in the face of the developmental contexts of her adult years. As Erikson has shown us, while the developmentally early powerfully persists, it yet persists in restated forms in the context of later developmental work.

The issue we must here confront is how we might conceive the developmental task of aging. In other words, how are we to understand those challenges that arise with aging within the context of which developmentally earlier processes, needs, and wishes are contextualized and restated? The following chapter offers a suggestion in this regard. In seeking to delineate this understanding we will be, in effect, reframing certain foundational aspects of the claim of the theological tradition that fulfillment with aging embodies continuing growth. More precisely, we will be reframing the way of understanding the *possibility* of growth.

CHAPTER 5

The Metaethical Task

INTENTIONALITY IN AGING

Several ministers gathered one evening to discuss the challenges posed in pastoral care with the aging. A middle-aged man, frustrated in his own efforts to address the needs of his older parishioners effectively, asked in exasperation: "Well, what do old people want, anyway?" At one level, of course, his exasperation is understandable. As an age group, older adults are as diverse, and possibly more so, than any other age group.[1] In this sense, there is no single answer possible to his question. Older adults are characterized by a plurality of wants and needs as are those of all ages. The mistaken aspect of the minister's question lay in his presumption that pastoral care with the aging should be easier, or at least more easily understood, given the similarities he believed accompanied being in "old age." Our ability to classify persons within a given chronological age range as being in their "old age," however, is potentially distorting in this respect: it reflects a convenience for us as well as an abstraction from the realities of the experience of aging itself.

Granting this, however, we can return to the minister's question from a different direction. We might ask if within this plurality of wants and needs there is a more general *intentionality* that tends to characterize the cohesing of the aging self. We can still ask, in other words, if there is a general developmental trend that tends to contextualize that diversity of wants and desires. In the terms we used at the conclusion of the previous chapter, is there a way of conceptualizing the challenges that frequently contextualize the diversity of the experience of aging?

In pastoral care we often assume a positive answer to these questions. Reverend Williams, for example, thought of the aging self as constituted primarily by the desire to withdraw from social obligation. The Church Life Committee discussed such ideas as coping with loss and the need to maintain relationships in this regard. Claims of a similar kind may be found in the theological tradition. Whether they lie at the focus or at the fringe of our thought, some prior understanding of the underlying intentionality of the aging self is almost inevitably a part of our interpretation of human fulfillment in aging.

The Developmental Task of Aging

Tell them what you have suffered by the deceits of sin; tell them the method and danger of temptation; tell them what you lost by delaying your repentance; and how God recovered you; and how the Spirit wrought upon your souls; tell them what comforts you have found in God; what safety and sweetness in a holy life; how sweet the holy scriptures have been to you; how prayers have prevailed; how the promises of God have been fulfilled. . . . Warn them to resist their fleshly lusts and to take heed of the ensnaring flatteries of sin; acquaint them truly with the history of public sins, and judgments, and mercies in the time which you have lived.[2]

In the above quotation Richard Baxter describes the work of old age in a manner that echoes much of the Christian theological tradition: the task of the aged is not only to continue a life of righteousness, but also to shore up, meditate on, and draw sustenance from the meaning of the righteous life as it has been enacted and lived in their lives. Implicitly throughout much of the theological tradition, there is a profound sense of aging as a time in which the question of the *meaning* of who one has become is raised to the fore by increasing closeness to death (and, of course, God's judgment) and the small and large traumas of loss and decay. Baxter's particular way of phrasing this may well strike us as optimistic. The "holy life" is unambiguously "sweet" and "safe" only for those who have been able to avoid taking it seriously. Nonetheless, while we may not be able to embrace all that was said, or the particular ways in which this idea has been cast in the tradition, we can see how the idea relates to some of the contemporary literature on aging. I will be seeking to illustrate one possible way of formulating that developmental task of aging which forms the restating and transforming context of a dialectically progressive understanding of growing older. In doing so, we will seem to move far from the way in which this idea was articulated in the theological tradition. Yet, I hope to show a certain similarity of concern.

I will be referring to this developmental challenge as the "metaethical task" of old age. The term "metaethics," of course, derives from moral philosophy. In that literature it is generally juxtaposed to normative ethics. Normative ethics is that aspect of moral philosophy that seeks to articulate those rules, principles, virtues, or character traits that are said to be morally good or bad, right or wrong. Thus, when we wonder under what circumstances we morally ought to tell the truth, for example, and seek to articulate the principles or rules that govern moral behavior in these circumstances, we are engaged in the task of normative ethics. Metaethics, on the other hand, is that aspect of moral philosophy that seeks to understand (at least in part) the meaning of our morally evaluative language. When we reflect on the meaning of "good" or "right" in their moral uses, we are engaged in metaethics. Metaethics, in this sense, is reflection on certain of the foundations of normative ethics.

The metaethical task perspective on aging is not a grand theory of aging, but rather an interpretative lens through which we may understand certain important psychic conflicts, human values, and psychological features of personality that a variety of human science theorists understand as characterizing old age. In this sense, it is a synthetic construct meant to capture some important—perhaps implicit—dimensions of what those theorists are suggesting. It is the metaethical task of aging that I will be suggesting as a contemporary restatement of certain aspects of the idea of growth with aging that plays such an important role in the theological tradition. Other aspects of the idea of growth with aging as found in the historic theological literature will be discussed in the following chapters.

To say that old age can be interpreted from a metaethical task perspective does not mean, of course, that the aged suddenly become academic moral philosophers concerned with sorting out the intricate analytic details of metaethics. It does mean, however, that we can conceptualize certain aspects of the aging process from the perspective of issues concerning the meaningfulness of the moral life, that is, of the particular formations one's moral becoming has taken. Thus, the metaethical task of old age refers to that process of dealing with—consciously and, probably for the most part, unconsciously—the meaningfulness (the "justification," if you will) of one's moral formation in the face of those internal and external threats to that formation that arise with aging. In order to begin to flesh out this perspective, I will suggest how the works of Erik Erikson and David Gutmann seem to suggest this orientation.

Two Developmental Theories

We can see this perspective illustrated most clearly in the work of Erikson. While we will be discussing Erikson's work more fully later, a few brief comments are in order at this point. In Erikson's life cycle theory, the developmental crisis which he calls integrity versus despair (the nuclear conflict of old age) follows that of generativity versus stagnation.[3] The significance of this lies in the fact that the crisis of generativity versus stagnation constitutes the normative center of his life cycle theory. It is with generativity that the psychological development of the self presses most fully beyond the individual to enabling the fulfillment of others (through procreative and productive activity). What can it mean, therefore, for Erikson to posit a developmental crisis that *follows* the normative center of his thought? A clue is provided by Lawrence Kohlberg's commentary on this situation:

> Erikson's ideal man has passed through his seventh stage of generativity and becomes an ethical man. . . . There remains for Erikson's man a task which is partly ethical, but more basically religious . . . a task . . . whose outcomes are a sense of integrity versus a sense of despair. The problem of integrity is not the problem of moral integrity, but the integrity of the meaning of the individual's life.[4]

The stage of generativity versus stagnation, in other words, involves principally a moral task. Upon the "resolution" of this conflict, therefore, the person must yet confront a crisis of meaning and, in particular, the meaning of his or her own moral becoming. In that this is a conflict which follows the primary stage of moral crisis and, indeed, raises the question of the continuing meaning of that normative center itself, we may say that Erikson's understanding of old age revolves around a "metaethical" task.

Other, more recent, theoretical formulations also seem conducive to the idea of a metaethical task perspective on aging. The psychologist Gutmann, for example, argues that some of what usually passes for deprivation and loss with aging may be seen instead as a response to maturational tendencies. Gutmann argues that through middle adulthood the life cycle is dominated by the "parental imperative." Indeed, in line with Erikson's concept of generativity, Gutmann believes that "parenthood seems to represent the point at which individual satisfaction intersects with species needs."[5] With the lapse of the parental imperative, however, the aged may acquire the capacity for further growth or maturation based on two developments.

The first of these has to do with transformations of cognitive capacities. What Gutmann has in mind here is that the aging may acquire the capacity to create and sustain meaningful object-relations even through relatively transient and insubstantial contact with the other. While the "other" may be persons (doctors, nurses, etc.), Gutmann argues that some older adults have the developmental capacity to make experientially substantial and powerfully real such "insubstantial" things as symbols and traditions. The second potential transformation Gutmann notes, echoing Carl Jung's understanding of development in the second half of life, has to do with the reemergence of certain gender-differentiated aspects of the personality that were necessarily repressed during the period of "chronic parental emergency." Thus, he says, older men may become more oriented toward passive-mastery of their environment and older women may become more oriented toward active-mastery.[6]

The core upon which both of these transformations turn, however, can be seen as the emergence of issues surrounding the meaning of one's moral (productive and reproductive) becoming—both with respect to the individual and the wider culture. On the individual level, the question of the meaningfulness of one's moral becoming is raised by the awareness of the transience of selfobjects (those objects, persons, etc., that are experienced as a part of the self) and by one's own decline. On the cultural level, the normative-ethical fabric of the culture—in Gutmann's view—must be held together by those very transformations. As Gutmann writes: "The aged provide, for all age groups, the transformative objects that facilitate the binding of narcissistic energies. They thus preserve the social order—the vulnerable skein of daily activities—from the destructive effects of excessive egotism and self-interest."[7] This interpretation of Gutmann's thought is far too brief to do justice to the richness of his formulations, but it may be sufficient to suggest how his work may be interpreted in line with the metaethical task perspective on old age.

Embracing the Metaethical Task

The works of Erikson and Gutmann are but two examples from the contemporary literature on aging that seem to imply a more general vision of the setting and import of old age within the life cycle—a general vision that I am here calling the "metaethical task perspective on old age." Certain aspects of the work of Kohlberg, K. Warner Schaie, and Margaret Lowenthal, I believe, also lend some support (at one level of abstraction or another) to this synthetic construct. We now need to be somewhat more specific about what the metaethical task of aging seems to imply, however. While our discussion in this section will be relatively abstract, we will move to more concrete examples of what this all means in the following sections.

Generative Concerns

First, the idea of the metaethical task of aging suggests that the period of life preceding old age is dominated by generative (productive and reproductive) concerns. The import of this is that the phase of development in which generative concerns constitute the organizing experiential matrix of the self is also understood as the normative core of the life cycle. It is seen, in other words, as the central period of integration of moral becoming.

The idea of "moral becoming," as I am using it, does not refer to the learning of particular moral rules or principles so much as the particular ways in which one comes (or not) to "care for" self and others. This is, at once, a moral and a psychological process and may be viewed from both an ethical and a psychological perspective. The idea of "moral becoming" may be seen from a psychological perspective as the way in which the self organizes its wants, needs, and desires in that period of life dominated by the requirements of expansion, extension, or transcendence of the self in productive and reproductive activity. From an ethical perspective, "moral becoming" refers to those principles of care which that very organizing expresses. In this chapter I am primarily concerned with it as a means of designating a psychological process. In this sense its dynamics are illuminated by Erikson's discussion of generativity versus stagnation, Gutmann's notion of the parental imperative, Schaie's discussion of "responsible" and "executive" cognitive styles in middle adulthood, etc.

While the metaethical task perspective on aging gives precedence in this developmental process to the period of life preceding old age, this is not to say that it is absent either before or after that period. Rather, as with Erikson, it is to say on the one hand that earlier development forms and is transformed by the process of integration of moral becoming in that period of life dominated by the primary cultural and biological avenues of such integration: parenthood and labor. On the other hand, while the dynamics of one's moral formation obviously continue into later adulthood, they are yet transformed and restated in the context of the metaethical task.

Meaning

From the metaethical task perspective, old age can only properly be understood within the above context; that is, as following the primary period of integration of moral becoming. As a second characteristic of this perspective, then, we can say that the period of life following the primary generative period raises the issues of the meaningfulness of the particular formations one's moral becoming has taken. This does not mean, of course, that older adults necessarily walk around talking about their past jobs or their children all the time. In its deeper sense, it has to do with the *meaning* of who one has become in the context of such generative issues (and in the context of one's full developmental history) and whether that meaning is sustaining in the light of the losses, challenges, and changes that accompany older adulthood.

Other Factors

Third, and finally, the metaethical task perspective on aging suggests that the way in which these issues are raised (and "resolutions" sought) reflects a variety of factors: the dynamics of one's previous life history, current biological and sociopsychological challenges, and developmental capacities that emerge with aging. In pastoral care with older adults our sorting out of these factors serves as diagnostic guideposts in understanding how older adults are coping with the metaethical task. In light of this it may prove useful to offer a tentative rereading of some of the oft-cited central dynamics of aging in order to clarify the way in which the metaethical task perspective on aging reframes our understanding of those dynamics. My point in doing this is not to analyze in detail the complexities that any of these dynamics present, but rather simply to outline how the metaethical task perspective might contextualize the way in which they are understood.

PSYCHOLOGICAL DYNAMICS

As a first example we can look at the psychological dynamics of grandparenthood in terms of how they function in relation to the metaethical task. Helene Deutsch and Therese Benedek observed several years ago that the experience of being a parent often revives unresolved conflicts from the parents' own childhood. In other words, the experience of caring for one's children as they confront the developmental issues of childhood and adolescence may raise for the parent conflicts surrounding those same issues from their own developmental history. In like manner, grandparenthood may evoke similar conflicts relative to one's own patterns of parenting. As Rebecca Cohen, Bertram Cohler, and Sidney Weissman have noted: "For the grandparental generation, observation of adult children with their own children evokes memories of their own child-rearing experiences, including concern that they may not have been good enough parents."[8] In the terms I am using in this essay, the way in which the metaethical task is raised (and "resolutions" sought) is relative to one's own moral becoming (in this case, one's own way of having been a parent). Grandparenthood, then, is far from a benign psychological experience: it may resurface the fantasies, guilt, joys, and disappointments of one's own moral becoming in adaptive or maladaptive ways with regard to the metaethical task.

A second frequently noted central dynamic of aging is the desire to maintain continuity and cohesiveness in the sense of self. Erikson has written of this in his discussion of the importance of "keeping things together" and maintaining a sense of wholeness in the face of those internal and external threats that arise with aging. Likewise, Morton Lieberman and Sheldon Tobin have recently argued that, under conditions of high stress (as in situations involving relocation to a nursing home), the psychology of aging may be dominated by this dynamic.[9] Certainly, the loss and threat of loss of—what Heinz Kohut calls—selfobjects (death of spouse and significant others, bodily decline, etc.) and the potential narcissistic injuries resulting from a changed position and role in society may well threaten, for some older adults, the fragmentation of the self.

The desire to maintain continuity and cohesiveness of the self is, as Kohut has shown, not unique to the aged.[10] Such self-dynamics function throughout life. Yet, the metaethical task perspective on aging suggests the restated context within which such dynamics function in old age. The dynamics of self-cohesion are contextualized by the issues surrounding the meaningfulness of one's moral becoming: can the meaning of who I have become be sustained and sustaining in a postgenerative phase of life?

A third central dynamic of aging is the oft-cited tendency of "turning inward" with aging. Older adults frequently experience an increased interiority: a greater focus on the self than on external events and objects. Bertram Cohler has suggested, for example, that "As a result of increased interiority, interest is lessened in maintaining social bonds, resulting in greater impatience with the necessity of caring for others."[11] How we are to read this is a difficult and controversial matter. Its probable relation to maintaining the cohesiveness of the self, particularly as nearness to death increases, must be clearly acknowledged. And, indeed, it is certainly consistent with the basic thrust of the metaethical task: the idea of a shift of central focus from moral becoming itself to the *meaning* of one's moral becoming. How the increased impatience in caring for others that Cohler ascribes to this process is to be read will be a topic for later discussion.

A fourth central dynamic of aging, as suggested by Robert Butler and Myrna Lewis, is the desire to leave a legacy. As they describe this process:

> This legacy may be children and grandchildren, work or art, personal possession, memories in the minds of others, even bodies or parts of them for use in medical research. Motivations for the tendency toward legacy are generally a combination of not wanting to be forgotten, of wanting to give of one's self magnanimously to those who survive, of wishing to remain in control in some way even after death (for example, through wills), of desiring to tidy up responsibly before death. Legacy provides a sense of continuity giving the older person a feeling of being able to participate even after death.[12]

This is, as Butler and Lewis note, closely related to the "elder" function of older adults: the "natural propensity of the old to share with the young the accumulated knowledge and experience they have collected."[13] From the metaethical task perspective on old age, the desire to leave a legacy and the "elder" function may be seen in part as avenues in the potential confirmation that one's moral becoming be seen by self and others as meaningful, as in some way making a continuing difference. Through a continuing participation in the ongoing cycle of generations, the sense of the meaningfulness of one's productive and reproductive becoming is potentially supported and nurtured.

Finally, a fifth frequently noted dynamic of aging is reminiscence and life review. The idea of life review, most systematically articulated by Butler, postulates a universal process precipitated by nearness to death wherein previously unresolved conflicts reemerge and which, if appropriately worked through, may lead to a new sense of serenity and well-being.[14] Reminiscence, as I am using it here, has to do with the more general tendency of older adults to draw on the personal past for the purpose of coping with current circumstances. The understanding of both these processes remains in its early stages at this point. As Lieberman and Tobin have suggested, however, the use of the personal past by older adults seems to serve a variety of purposes, some of which have to do with dealing with unresolved conflicts, others—perhaps more frequently—having to do with the dramatization of the personal past to create a sustaining sense of self. As they write of the latter, "the elderly more often rework their personal past for the defense of a meaningful self-concept."[15]

The metaethical task perspective on aging asks us to see life review and reminiscence, at least in part, as resources for the validation or modification of the meaning of one's moral becoming. Nearness to death, severity of current stress, and more general psychological and biological dynamics may all come into play in terms of the way in which the personal past is used and the extent to which the meaning of one's moral becoming is transformed, sustained, or "mythicized." Yet, the metaethical task perspective on aging suggests that many of these dynamics take place in the context of the question of the continuing meaning of one's moral becoming and the extent to which it can be sustained and sustaining in later adulthood.

THE METAETHICAL TASK AND
THE PROBLEM OF HOPE

The way in which the metaethical task perspective contextualizes each of these dynamics of aging points to an underlying issue: the problem of hope. The question of whether the meaning of one's moral becoming can be sustained and sustaining in later adulthood, in other words, is a restatement and transformation of that primordial struggle of the self to achieve a sense of the possibility of its own efficacy in a world which can confirm that possibility, that is, the sense of hope. As Erikson describes the ego strength of hope in early infancy: "Hope is the enduring belief in the attainability of primal wishes, in spite of the dark urges and rages which mark the beginnings of existence and leave a lasting residue of threatening Estrangement."[16] Within the perspective of the metaethical task, indeed, *fulfillment* in old age is the consummation of that primordial hope that marks the beginnings of life. It is, in part, the hope that who I have become and who I am now becoming can allow me to continue to realize values important to me even in the midst of bodily decay and increasing closeness to death.

Erikson has argued that this struggle with hope underlying the metaethical task has a religious dimension:

> Every human being's Integrity may be said to be religious (whether explicitly or not). Each person engages in an inner search for, and a wish to communicate with, that mysterious, that Ultimate Other: for

there can be no "I" without an "Other" and no "We" without a shared "Other." That, in fact, is the first revelation of the life cycle when the maternal person's eyes shiningly recognize us even as we begin to recognize her. It is also the hope of old age, according to St. Paul's promise.[17]

In this sense, fulfillment in aging entails the affirmation of those hope- and trust-infusing foundations of existence that make one's moral becoming meaningful, and indeed, possible at all.

The concern with hope in old age pervades the historic theological literature as well. The emphasis in part was on hope in eternal life as a salve for elderly troubled by their decline. Thus, for example, John Calvin wrote that "by meditating on that renovation which is laid up as the object of our hope, we may, with tranquil minds, suffer this frail tabernacle to be dissolved."[18] Likewise, the American Puritan theologian William Bridge wrote:

> What then, though your turf house now be ready to fire into a fever with every spark of distemper, is there not enough in that house above to pay for all? Surely there is. Why then should ye not lift up your heads, ye old men, and be of good comfort under all your natural infirmities.[19]

Yet this emphasis often does not seem to have been merely a medication for troubled souls. It was frequently, as well, a way of lessening the potential concern about the meaninglessness of the trials of aging and, thereby, of encouraging the elderly to continue in the righteous life. The hope of old age was tied in part, in other words, to the idea of the continuing possibility of realizing values central to the Christian life. In this sense, there is an area of common concern (the possibility of continuing to realize important values) regarding the problem of hope in older adulthood in the contemporary metaethical task perspective and the Christian theological tradition. Yet, there is at least one important difference in focus as well.

Erikson, for example, is primarily concerned with the "religious" dimension of hope as a psychological phenomenon. Yet, we must also ask the question Erikson does not address: *Are* the foundations of existence in fact hope- and trust-infusing? We must surely realize upon reflection that such hope is radically underjustified simply within the terms of the history of our own lives or the history of our world. Is the psychological necessity for such an affirmation, then, a final tragicomic gesture in a world which at its roots is, at best, indifferent to our longing? Is the consummation of hope in old age a last defiant cry to no One at all and, thus, an illusion or mistake, however emotionally advantageous? Or, to put it another way, if our pastoral care with the aging seeks to confirm the hope of old age are we but hucksters of psychological necessity or do we in fact believe that the foundations of existence *are* hope- and trust-infusing? And what could it really mean if we think they are? Without denying the psychological-developmental character of hope, these questions push us to consider another dimension of hope: hope as a limiting and structuring dimension of human existence. I shall return to these questions in this regard in the final chapter.

PASTORAL CARE AND THE
METAETHICAL TASK

The metaethical task of aging is, as I have said, an interpretation of that vision of the nature and place of old age in the life cycle that seems to underlie several contemporary human science theories of the aging process. It suggests an interpretation of that underlying intentionality of the aging self that frequently contextualizes conscious and unconscious dimensions of the diversity of central dynamics of growing older. What does this mean, however, with respect to pastoral care? To put it succinctly, it suggests that conflicts within or between the central dynamics of aging are often expressions of the inability to construe the meaning of one's moral becoming in a manner sustaining to the aging self. The causes of such inability must be sought in the dynamic interplay of intrapsychic, biological, and sociocultural factors. Part of the task of pastoral care, then, with regard to this aspect of aging, is (1) to facilitate appropriate meaning-making with respect to the challenges of the metaethical task and (2) to facilitate a value-consensus within the community that encourages and sustains such appropriate meaning-making. A few brief comments on each of these may be suggestive in terms of how this aspect of pastoral care with the aging might be conceived.

Pastoral care with the aging involves facilitating appropriate meaning-making with regard to the metaethical task. The metaethical task presents a challenge of growth, development, or maturation for the aging self. It is a challenge that many older adults negotiate with little difficulty (or, at least, little consciously expressed difficulty). For others, however, past maladaptation and/or current stresses may create profound conflicts focused on the metaethical task. Margaret Arnold's effort to maintain the continuity and cohesiveness of her self, for example, was threatened by—among other things—the emergence of previously repressed aspects of her personality. The truncation of her moral becoming (in its relation to her passive experience of herself, her hysteric mode of adaptation to the Oedipal situation of her childhood, and the psychic consequences of consistent selfobject failure) left her badly confused and distraught with regard to the metaethical task. Part of the task of pastoral care in such situations is to enable older adults appropriately to reconceptualize the meaning of their moral becoming. Whether this would entail, in any particular case, an explicit reworking of conflicts, "mythologizing," or shoring up crumbling defenses is a matter for careful and sensitive pastoral judgment.

Pastoral care with the aging involves facilitating the building of a value-consensus within the community which encourages and sustains such appropriate meaning-making. We must not overlook in our discussion the ways in which social and cultural factors affect efforts to deal with the metaethical task. Certainly, conflicts between the central dynamics of aging may be generated or influenced by such factors. For example, the culturally legitimated avenues of self-cohesion and self-continuity with aging may become so narrowed as to conflict with the desire to leave a legacy or the "elder" function. As Parker Palmer has written, "We need to remember again and again, that many of our private problems are really public issues."[20] In other words, pastoral care needs to be ever aware of the ways in which the disordered inwardness of some older adults may be related to the disordered character of public life. I suspect that much of what we usually understand as emotional distress due to the losses of aging is a result, not simply of the losses themselves, but of the loss of a meaningful cultural context in and through which individuals age. As Gutmann has put it, there must be a "coordination between the developmental 'givens' and the value consensus of the society which 'receives' them."[21] To put this another way, pastoral care must be ever aware of those disjunctions between the metaethical task and the value-consensus of the community, whereby the metaethical task lacks appropriate cultural (public) meaning.

A minister of a small urban church, for example, was complaining that several of the older members of her congregation seemed to be overly argumentative and negative about church activities and programs. She attributed this to the condition of "being old" and thought that private counsel with each of these persons was the only hope for resolution. While there can be no doubt that the expressions of dissatisfaction reflected individual circumstances, one must also consider the possibility that such negative modes of expression were "perceived" by the older members to be the only avenues available for expressing the deeper disjunction between the developmental challenges of older adulthood and the value-consensus of the church community.

As with the minister of this congregation, our initial response to the "problems of aging" is likely to be along instrumental-technological lines: federal or local programs of relief or pastoral counsel are professed to relieve this or that dimension of the problem. It is certainly not unusual for these programs to do some good. To provide food and medical care or spiritual guidance to older adults in need of such is obviously a good thing. Yet, such programs more often than not do nothing to change the underlying cultural problem and, indeed, by providing the success of short-run relief, often serve to legitimate the deeper disorder.

The point in all this is that pastoral care with the aging cannot understand its task only within the realm of individuals, or even groups of individuals. Pastoral care finally involves care for public life. This may very well seem odd today. Is not the real point of pastoral care in the trenches of individual psyches? Many of us engaged in pastoral care must yet discover that the point of it all lies not in the consulting room, but in the nature and direction of the life made possible in the world community. But, then, one must not underestimate, I suppose, the excitement and seduction of the trenches.

SUMMARY

Since we have traveled a long and circuitous route in the last two chapters, it may be helpful to recapitulate briefly where we are at this point. Much of the historic Christian theological literature suggested that fulfillment in aging was marked by continuing growth. Part of its justification for this claim, however, sometimes entailed a tendency toward an anthropological dualism. I have argued that this understanding of human nature can no longer meaningfully be maintained. I also argued that the idea of growth with aging cannot adequately be supported by an undialectically progressive position with respect to human development. If the idea of growth with aging is to make sense, I suggested, it must be explicated within the context of a dialectical progressivism.

In this chapter I have suggested one possible way of articulating certain of the developmental or maturational challenges of aging. The notion of the metaethical task of old age suggests that there is a developmental process (or, if you will, a possibility of growth or maturation) in later adulthood. This perspective, of course, may well seem to have taken us a long way from the theological tradition. In some ways this is quite true. The metaethical task perspective on aging is obviously not precisely what Calvin or Baxter or John Chrysostom had in mind. What we can say about the relation of the metaethical task perspective to the discussion of growth in the historic theological literature is more circumspect: it is a representation, in certain of the language of the latter half of the twentieth century, of a particular aspect of the idea of growth with aging as found in the theological literature. Given the necessity of reframing certain foundational assumptions about human nature, the metaethical task restates certain aspects of the notion of growth with aging in that changed context. If nothing else, this interpretation of some of the contemporary human science literature on aging may hint that the emphasis in the theological literature on growth in the face of loss and decline in the later years of life may itself perhaps meaningfully be restated and reformulated in our time. Yet we are far from being able to say even that with much clarity at this point, and it is to further issues in this regard that we must now turn.

CHAPTER 6

The Moral Praxis
of Aging

In the previous chapter we examined how the intentionality of the aging self might be conceptualized. Our images of fulfillment with aging obviously embody more than a descriptive claim about the nature of the aging process, however. They also entail an ethical claim—a claim often implied in discussions of "healthy" or "adaptive" or "successful" ways of aging. This sort of thing is a claim about the moral praxis of the aging self: a claim about what principles, standards, values, or virtues ought to be expressed in the self's organizing of itself with aging. To put this another way, the question of the meaning of growth with aging in the face of loss and decline is only in part a psychological question, it is also a moral one.

THE QUESTION OF VALUES

Ours, of course, is an age of increasingly unashamed prudence. Robert Gray and David Moberg have written:

> Both the teachings of America's religions and the values of her social scientists include the goal of making old age a time of happiness and joy, a stage of good personal and social adjustment, an age of high morale, and a time of life satisfaction, rather than a period of mental anguish, social maladjustment, and dissatisfaction.[1]

Such values as high morale, life satisfaction, and personal adjustment in old age seem to be self-evident and sufficient in themselves. What are we to make of this, however, with respect to the Christian witness? It is hard to deny that an adequate interpretation of the Christian witness would probably not be for mental anguish, social maladjustment, and dissatisfaction in old age. It is probably even true that it will desire happiness, joy, and life satifaction for the aging. But, then, who is *for* mental anguish and *against* happiness in old age? The very triviality of this way of putting it suggests that a deeper dilemma is being obscured. That dilemma forms the central question of this chapter: How ought we to conceive the moral praxis of aging?

For many today, including some in pastoral care and the helping professions generally, the question we will be addressing in this chapter may seem irrelevant or, worse, dangerous if not rendered trivial. The quite appropriate concern with moralism in pastoral care has often tended to make such discussions confessional melting pots of least-common-denominator values. Yet, for John Chrysostom, Ambrose, John Calvin, Richard Baxter, and others in the Christian tradition, the idea of growth with aging clearly embodied a rather stronger interpretation of the moral praxis of aging. In other words, the notion of "growth" in old age was filled out and made determinant in a specifically religioethical form.

I will be arguing in this chapter that the question of moral praxis is *not* a peculiarity of the theological or the premodern interpretation of aging, but rather an inevitable dimension of the interpretation of aging. Neither Mrs. Arnold's pastoral counselor, nor the Church Life Committee planning programming for the older members of the congregation, nor even the social scientist seeking to determine what constitutes "successful" aging, can but implicate particular moral assumptions about what virtues or principles ought to be expressed in the self's organizing of itself with aging.

It is now fairly widely accepted that human science theories of the aging process are not only "reports" of the "evidence," but also particular ways of construing what they understand as counting as evidence. This representation of the aging process in human science theories of aging expresses certain foundational assumptions (or conceptual moral constraints) about human wants and needs and about appropriate and inappropriate ways of organizing those wants and needs. In light of this, as the philosopher Charles Taylor has noted about human science interpretation in general, they embody a particular "value slant."[2] In other words, theories of the aging process express, either explicitly or implicitly, practical moral intention.

Robert Kastenbaum's lament, cited in chapter 2, concerning the failure of the human science literature on aging to address the "practical moral" issues, then, is only partially correct. The problem is not that the human sciences have not and do not promulgate moral visions in their theories of aging, but rather that these moral visions are rarely acknowledged and, even more rarely, critically analyzed on the normative grounds they imply.

PASTORAL CARE AND
THE MORAL PRAXIS OF AGING

This is an important point for those engaged in pastoral care with older adults to have firmly in mind: our interventions always involve an understanding of the moral praxis of aging. These understandings may or may not make sense on moral grounds, they may adequately or inadequately re-present the moral dimensions of the Christian witness. We cannot really know unless we take the time to work them out. Unfortunately, the seduction of technique in pastoral care often tends to obscure awareness of the practical-moral character of what one is doing in employing this or that therapeutic tool. A brief example may help to clarify this.

There is a growing literature today on the use of behavior-modification techniques in nursing homes for the aged. One oft-cited use involves the reinforcing of proper eating habits (with utensils rather than fingers) through the presentation or withholding of reinforcers—such as food—so as to shape the appropriate behavior. Not surprisingly, there is a high rate of success with the technique (it is amazing, is it not, what some people will do so as not to go hungry?). One sometimes gets the impression, however, that the therapy involved here is more either for the nurses and staff of the home (who no longer have to clean up after the residents) or for the residents' relatives (who no longer have to witness this decay of civility) rather than the residents themselves. What, one needs to ask, does this sort of thing say about the moral praxis of aging?

I am not implying in this that *any* use of behavioral techniques is necessarily problematic. For that matter, other therapeutic techniques generate their own problems in this regard as well. My point, rather, is that the interpretive lens that guides the appropriation of particular therapeutic techniques inevitably expresses a practical

moral intention which subsequently informs the nature and direction of the helping relationship.

Our practical moral intentions, of course, also influence other
forms of pastoral care with the elderly: how we understand Christian education with older adults, how various forms of "retirement
rituals" are celebrated in the church, how we make sense of celebrat-
ing the Eucharist with elderly shut-ins, how we choose the types of
sermons we preach at retirement or nursing homes, etc. In all these
situations, some understanding of the moral praxis of aging forms
(and is formed by) our pastoral care. Part of that interpretive lens
that focuses our way of seeing older adults and our tasks and responsibilities with regard to them is made up precisely by certain (more or
less clear) images of the moral praxis of aging.

While acknowledging the existence of such "value orientations,"
some of us in pastoral care have difficulty accepting what this really
means. Having effectively abandoned our practical theological tradition in any meaningful sense, we have thrown in our lot with the
human sciences. In acknowledging that the human sciences are not
value-neutral (and that they cannot be so), pastoral care may again
seem subject to what Richard Bernstein has called that Cartesian
Anxiety for lack of an Archimedian point.[3] In other words, pastoral
care may seem to lose its only firm, discursively redeemable founda-
tion. This concern arises in part, however, because of the failure to
understand pastoral care within the context of a truly practical
(practical-moral) theology.[4] To say that the interpretation of aging
necessarily entails a moral dimension, however, is not license to do
whatever one "feels" like in pastoral care, but rather a call to serious
practical reflection.

THE MORAL PRAXIS OF AGING
IN THE CHRISTIAN
THEOLOGICAL TRADITION

In much of the historical Christian theological literature, as I
observed earlier in this essay, the idea of growth with aging referred
to continuing advance in the Christian life: progress in establishing a
right relation to God. As I have said, this meant at least two things:
first, it meant that the aged were to be especially concerned with
repentance and meditation. These things were seen as important in

progressing in a right relation to God since they strengthened the soul (and, probably, convinced one of the necessity for further repentance) by recalling God's mercy, forgiveness, and blessings throughout the course of one's life.

Second, the historic literature often understood the religioethical witness of age to require carrying out certain responsibilities to others. In particular, it was deemed important for the aged to seek to advance the progress of the younger generations in their own love of God and neighbor. Age, as Friedrich Schleiermacher wrote, "must serve as protection to the seed of future generations, and it is a gift that every creature must offer in order that the rest of nature may receive his life."[5] Some theologians tempered this emphasis by suggesting that the very old—those especially close to death—could retire somewhat from some of the demands of earlier old age. In the graphic language of William Bridge:

> If a tooth be to be drawn, and the gum be cut, the tooth doth come out with ease; but if it be fast set in the gum, and not first loosened from the gum, it comes out with much difficulty: and why is the reason that many die with such difficulty: because they are so fast set in their worldly gums, they are not loosened from their relations. Good therefore it is for old men who are upon the brink of death, to cut their gum, and to loosen themselves from this world and all their relations.[6]

Thus, while it was seen as appropriate for those particularly close to death to withdraw from the world, by far the greater part of old age was not to be marked by disengagement from the world. The underlying idea, as I have said, was a profound sense of the interconnection of the generations: the fulfillment of each was connected with, and required promoting, the fulfillment of others. The focus of the moral praxis of aging in all this, then, was on the individual in relational context: in relation to that one Other whose purposes must be one's own and in relation to those many others whose lives form a part of one's own.

In this sense, old age was seen as a continuation of the Christian life in general. While older adults were clearly seen to have special needs and unique opportunities, these were understood within the overarching rubric of the Christian life: humans in relation to God called to a life of love of God and of mediating that love to others. *What tended to change, in other words, was not these most basic life patterns, but rather the way in which these patterns were to be expressed given the realities and challenges of older adulthood.* The form of expression, not the content, of Christian agape was seen to change somewhat with aging. Growth with aging, therefore, meant growth with regard to the most basic elements of the Christian life. The relational focus of the moral praxis of aging in much of the historic Christian theological literature assured the continuing importance of other-regarding actions in old age.

Understandings of the moral praxis of aging are found, as I have said, not only in the Christian theological tradition. In television programs, advertisements, political party platforms, human science interpretations of aging, contemporary literature, and in many other places, we find a myriad of possible images of how the self ought to organize itself with aging. These images, in often subtle ways, influence the pastoral care of the church with the aging. Some of these images, of course, are more compatible with the historic theological literature than others. Some are profoundly different. Given the plurality of possibilities available in our world, which seems relatively more adequate? And why? Does the emphasis in the historic theological literature still make sense or must it give way to something else? In order to think through these questions, I will isolate two alternative images of the moral praxis of aging prominent today.

TWO IMAGES OF AGING

The Compliance of Necessary Victims

The first example I have chosen is most characteristic of the "aging as loss" paradigm. The moral praxis of aging in this orientation circles around a "necessary victim" perspective. Since loss defines old age and since this loss is irremedial, the moral praxis of aging is characterized by the morality of marginalization: so long as the paternalistic functions of representatives of the broader culture (ministers, doctors, lawyers, etc.) are paid due heed, the aged may squeeze whatever joy they wish out of life within the limits of civility. Of course, the limits of civility tend to be much narrower for the aged than for other age groups (as in matters of sexuality, for example) but, then, victims—and expecially necessary victims—have little room to quibble.

The central value or "virtue" to be expressed in the self's organizing of itself with aging from this perspective is compliance or deference. The rationalization for this is frequently grounded in the perceived powerlessness of the aged in the face of irreversible loss and decline. In practice, this is often extended as their increasing powerlessness in general. The insidious quality of this is reflected in the apparent exceptions: those older adults who struggle to maintain some sense of power are perceived as, again, "necessary victims" (suffering from senility, etc.), albeit obnoxious ones.

An overarching "aging as loss" orientation often promotes a moral praxis which seeks to obscure the psychological and social factors within which it functions. To put it most forthrightly, the "aging as loss" definition of old age frequently functions within individual, familial, and social matrices of power and domination in their relation to culturally legitimated avenues of self-cohesion and identity. This can all be made to sound mighty humanitarian, of course. Etiquette often demands that domination don a more paternalistic guise.

Historically, as Keith Thomas has noted, the conflict between the younger and older generations was fought (consciously and unconsciously) over access to power and to material resources: land, marriage, autonomy, career, etc.[7] In this sense, with regard to the younger generations, the "aging as loss" paradigm accurately reflected the wish. At present, of course, at least the material bases of the conflict seem largely to have become inverted due to the decline of gerontocracy in the West, and the cultural legitimation of the productive obsolescence of the aged. The best one can say for this inversion, however, is that at times the results have been ambiguous.

This understanding of the moral praxis of aging will strike most of us as punitive and unjust. This is so for at least three reasons. First, it subordinates the needs and wishes of the aged themselves to the needs and wishes of those who presently happen to enjoy the fruits of power and advantage. This fundamental moral asymmetry between persons, however, cannot be justified simply by the appeal to possession of power or advantage itself since it can always be questioned whether the uses to which those things are put are morally justifiable. The mere possession of power or advantage, in other words, does not morally justify the uses to which they are put. Second, the uses to which power and advantage are put in this understanding of the moral praxis of aging are untenable as well. Such fundamental moral notions as freedom and justice, not to mention Christian agape, are played havoc with here. This is not to say that paternalism is never justified. Certain losses that occasionally accompany aging may indeed warrant such a position. But to make this claim requires, at least in part, an empirical assessment concerning the severity of the loss and decline. Thus, third, while the physiological losses of aging may occasionally be severe, simply defining aging as loss (the empirical claim upon which this position frequently rests) is untenable, as suggested in the last chapters. In other words, the understanding of the intentionality of the aging self which often undergirds this position is inadequate.

Normative Individualism

An alternative way of conceiving the moral praxis of aging, and one that seems to be gaining a good deal of impetus today, might be called "normative individualism." The moral praxis of aging in this orientation is usually encircled by a subjective-individualist orientation. The criteria of adequacy for the self's organizing of itself with aging, in other words, are principally those of the individual's sense of well-being or satisfaction or personal adjustment. To say that this is an individualist orientation is simply to note that criteria other than those of individuals' own experience of themselves are usually excluded.

This orientation is found not only in certain aspects of the gerontological literature, but in the general culture as well. Some aspects of popular culture, for example, encourage older adults simply to "do their own thing" or "do whatever makes you happy." Likewise, the ethos of some upper-middle-class retirement communities is permeated with a similar tone: what Maggie Kuhn once called the "playpen" approach to aging. One of the clearest, most systematic examples of this orientation, however, is in the gerontological literature on "successful aging." It will repay us, therefore, to examine this literature more closely.[8]

One of the questions gerontologists have long been concerned with is what fosters "successful aging." What is it that enables a "good old age"? This question has been understood to have obvious programmatic import for the helping professions: if we know what enables persons to age successfully, these conditions can be implemented in the appropriate settings. Thus, the programmatic dimensions of this concern generate questions in technical reason: what are the most appropriate and efficacious means to enable successful aging? In other words, what programs, workshops, situational restructuring, therapeutic interventions, and the like, ought we to implement in our churches, our nursing homes, our governmental service agencies, or our pastoral care so as to enable older adults to age successfully? The "ought" here, of course, is the "ought" of technical rationality, that is, the criteria of the "ought" are those of technical reason: efficiency, efficacy, etc.

This all may seem straightforward enough. Yet, upon reflection we must surely realize that the question of the *means* of enabling successful aging only makes sense if we know to what *successful* aging refers. At this level, the question of successful aging is clearly value-laden and any particular articulation of its meaning will embody a distinct moral structure, that is, in effect, an interpretation of the moral praxis of aging. Many of the measures that have been devised for successful aging in the gerontological literature imply a normative individualistic ethic. In order to suggest how this understanding of the moral praxis of aging gets worked out in this literature, I will illustrate with one example: the Life Satisfaction Index (LSI).

A CASE STUDY: THE LIFE
SATISFACTION INDEX

An early, but still influential and widely discussed, example of measures of successful aging in the gerontological literature is the Life Satisfaction Index developed by Bernice Neugarten, Robert Havighurst, and Sheldon Tobin for use in the Kansas City studies of older adults in the late 1950s.[9] The authors of the LSI acknowledge that all such procedures entail implicit value judgments. They maintain, however, that "once the investigator makes his value judgments explicit by the choice of his terms and his criteria, furthermore, the actual construction and validation of such a measure can go forward in relatively straightforward and value-neutral manner."[10] This perspective on the problem, though, tends to short-circuit the real issues raised by the acknowledgement of the necessary existence of value judgments in such measures. In particular, it leaves unresolved the question of the relative adequacy, on normative-ethical grounds, of the index generated by those values. With just a little searching, however, the moral structure of the LSI becomes clear.

The LSI was constructed from five scales: zest and apathy, resolution and fortitude, congruence between desired and achieved goals, self-concept, and mood tone. Since all five scales contain implicit values, brief comments on two may be sufficient to suggest the general thrust of the LSI's moral structure. The first scale, zest and apathy, enables the observer to rank the individual from a score of five (high zest) to a score of one (apathy). As Neugarten, Havighurst, and Tobin cite the characteristics required of the older person to be ranked at the highest end of the scale: "Speaks of several activities and relationships with enthusiasm. Feels that 'now' is the best time of life. Loves to do things, even sitting at home. Takes up new activities, makes new friends readily, seeks self-improvement. Shows zest in several areas of life."[11] The lowest score is given to those who "live on the basis of routine [and who do not] think anything worth doing."[12] Human fulfillment with aging ("successful aging") here necessitates a life of enthusiastic involvement. It is important to note though that the focus of "zest" is the individual herself. It is "keeping oneself busy." It does not necessarily entail (it is optional that it might) active concern for others. This has the practical effect of a normative individualism in that the emphasis is on the individual's activity itself and not on the impact of this activity on anyone or anything else.

This same normative individualist quality is revealed in other scales as well. For example, as Neugarten, Havighurst, and Tobin define the scale "congruence between desired and achieved goals": "The extent to which [the individual] feels he has achieved his goals in life, whatever these goals might be; feels he has succeeded in accomplishing what he regards as important."[13] Thus, to use one of their examples, if an elderly thief believes he has succeeded in meeting his goals for thievery, he would, on the criteria of this scale, be identified as a "successful" ager. Again, it is the individual's own goals and the experience of whether they were accomplished or not that is the criterion of successful aging. Human fulfillment, in this scheme, does not consist in a universalized normative content of action, but rather in a universalized experience accompanying whatever action is done, that is, in the feeling of well-being.

The LSI and, indeed, most measures of successful aging in the gerontological literature, are simply one type of example of normative individualist understanding of the moral praxis of aging today. Yet it does help us see the general vision normative individualism implies as an interpretation of the moral praxis of aging. While the LSI is not a pastoral care tool per se, similar normative individualist images frequently arise in that context. Reverend Williams, in his interaction with the Andersons, for example, clearly evinced a normative individualistic ethic. While he seems to have ascribed to the "aging as loss" paradigm, his interpretation of the moral praxis of aging was less that of "compliance" than that of normative individualism: emphasizing, as he did, the importance of the Andersons' own enjoyment and relaxation and his failure to put this emphasis in any relational context.

PROBLEMS OF NORMATIVE
INDIVIDUALISM

The emphasis on individual satisfaction or well-being in normative individualism is, in some ways, an important corrective to the "necessary victim" perspective found in certain articulations of the "aging as loss" paradigm. It seeks to effect an incorporation of the moral praxis of aging into a more culturally central alternative. Yet, finally, it is neither sufficient in itself nor an adequate means of re-presenting the Christian witness with respect to aging. There are two reasons for this judgment.

First, in collapsing the meaning of the moral praxis of aging into the individual's sense of satisfaction, normative individualism tends to encourage two psychological configurations potentially dangerous to the aged in contemporary society: (1) an increased emphasis on stringent self-boundaries and (2) an increased emphasis on the centrality and uniqueness of the individual. As David Gutmann has argued, contemporary society is marked by a widening arena of individuals who are perceived as strangers and a narrowing of affiliational bonds along increasingly cruder egocentric lines.[14] It is less and less unusual in our time even for our neighbors to be strangers to us. Who counts within our sense of "we" seems to have become increasingly delimited. Gutmann's point here is not necessarily that people are more "narcissistic" than in previous times (though his language leans heavily in that direction at times). Rather, the critical issue is the more subtle point that contemporary life fosters relatively primitive forms of narcissism and that the culture and institutions of our time seldom provide either the rationale or the structures which might enable the transformation to more developed forms of narcissism. That is, to use Heinz Kohut's terms, narcissism could take more mature forms of idealization and grandiosity. In the present situation, however, the aged and other vulnerable groups are at increased risk either from neglect or abuse. Gutmann notes that urban culture is less and less able to shape narcissism to the collective weal. Egocentricity becomes characteristic, leading to associations "not according to the 'social' and generation-transcending categories of family and class, but according to the most visible and tangible categories of skin color, sex (or sexual preference), and age. The motto of affiliation becomes, 'I love those who are, indisputably, most like myself.'"[15] In other words, while normative individualism seeks to incorporate the moral praxis of aging into a more culturally central alternative than that provided by the "aging as loss" paradigm, it may actually covertly compound the problem by reinforcing a mutual psychological alienation between the aged and the broader community.

Second, a normative individualist understanding of the moral praxis of aging tends to see object-relations as incidental to rather than constitutive of the person. In doing so, it implies that such relations are to be seen as but means (however necessary) to individuals satisfaction. By focusing its attention so sharply on the self's experience of itself in relative isolation from these relations, it implies a secondary and instrumental quality to them. As an interpretation of the moral praxis of aging, then, this perspective implicitly encourages older adults to see other people as merely means to the achievement of their own sense of happiness. Clearly, Christian agape and more general moral philosophical considerations would rule out this sort of vision.

THE RELATIONAL UNDERSTANDING
OF MORAL PRAXIS

What both of these problems point to is the necessity of conceiving the moral praxis of aging in a relational manner. It is precisely this understanding of the moral praxis of the aging self to which the historic theological literature points as well. In purely formal terms, the relational understanding of the moral praxis of aging suggests that the central value in the self's organizing of itself with aging is the form of the self's relation to others as well as to itself. But does this make sense today? While I have already suggested the relatively greater adequacy of this perspective on ethical grounds, we must still wonder whether it makes sense with respect to developmental processes in later adulthood. While the broader questions this issue raises are beyond our scope in this space, it may prove useful simply to illustrate two contemporary resources within the human sciences for understanding the relational ground of the moral praxis of aging.

Erik Erikson

A first contemporary resource in understanding the relational ground of the moral praxis of aging is found in the work of Erik Erikson. In Erikson's life cycle theory, the dominant psychosocial challenge of aging is defined by the nuclear conflict of integrity versus despair. As Erikson has described the syntonic element integrity:

> This in its simplest meaning is, of course, a sense of *coherence* and *wholeness* that is, no doubt, at supreme risk under such terminal conditions as include a *loss of linkages* in all three organizing processes: in the Soma, the pervasive weakening of tonic interplay in connecting tissues, blood-distributing vessels, and the muscle system; in the Psyche, the gradual loss of mnemonic coherence in experience, past and present; and in the Ethos, the threat of a sudden and nearly total loss of responsible function in generative interplay. What is demanded here could simply be called "integrality," a tendency to keep things together.[16]

An important part of what such coherence involves for Erikson is the acceptance of finitude and limitation. This acceptance extends to the recognition of the relativity of the very style of integrity of which the individual partakes. Integrity involves the acceptance that one's culturally mediated style of integrity is relative to the historical coincidence (time and place) of one's existence. Yet, while aware of the relativity of one's own particular style of integrity, "the possessor of integrity is ready to defend the dignity of his own life against all physical and economic threats."[17]

The dystonic element in this nuclear conflict is despair: "the feeling that the time is short, too short for the attempt to start another life and to try out alternate roads to integrity."[18] Erikson conceives despair, like the dystonic elements of all the nuclear conflicts, as a natural reaction to the psychosocial challenges of the particular stage of life. Even under the best of circumstances, despair remains the ever-present counterpoint of integrity.

The ego strength or virtue that Erikson sees as arising from the successful balancing of integrity and despair in old age is wisdom. The concept of wisdom, much like that of integrity, remains fairly diffuse in Erikson's work. He provides no systematic articulation of its meaning. Its principal characteristic, however, is an integrated heritage or tradition that the older adult lives and conveys to the oncoming generations. Whereas generative care is the active concern for what has been generated, wisdom is "detached concern with life itself in the face of death itself. . . . It responds to the need of the oncoming generation for an integrated heritage and yet remains aware of the relativity of knowledge."[19] Wisdom, like integrity in Erikson's perspective, is generally not an individualistic achievement, but rather connotes the individual's participation in, and transmission to others of, a wider cultural wisdom.

Erikson's use of the concept of wisdom provides something of a complement to that of integrity. While integrity entails a turn inward, wisdom suggests a new and different concern for the cycle of generations. In the emergence of integrity and through a lived wisdom, the future possibility of meaningful life for the oncoming generations, as well as the integrity of the individual's own life, is made possible. Human fulfillment in old age for Erikson, as for the theological tradition, requires understanding the moral praxis of aging in this relational context.

Adaptive-Evolutionary Analyses

A second resource for understanding the relational ground of the moral praxis of aging is found in what may well seem an unlikely area: certain adaptive-evolutionary analyses of developmental processes. Some, of course, suggest that old age is the one period of life that is irrelevant from the adaptive-evolutionary perspective. In other words, old age is but the "running out" of the genetic program. In this sense, old age has no adaptive significance (in the sense of being subject to evolutionary processes) for the species. According to P. S. Timiras, however, when natural selection leads to a life span beyond the reproductive years, this is not necessarily only incidental to some earlier effect. In a highly sociable and educable species, such as the human species, the lengthened life may be due to some benefit conferred by the infertile on the fertile.[20] What Timiras is suggesting is that while the individual may no longer contribute directly to the genetic pool, that individual may yet contribute to the enhancement of the survival of those who can still reproduce. Thus, particular characteristics or traits of the aged may have been selected through the evolutionary process given their contribution to socio-cultural (and, mediately, biological) adaptive-evolutionary processes.

James Birren has made a similar suggestion within the context of his "counterpoint" theory of aging and evolution.[21] The sociobiologist David Barash has even put the matter into the context of sociobiological discussions of altruism.[22] The evolutionary rationales presented by Timiras, Birren, and Barash, then, center on the potential contributions of the aged to the younger generations. Indeed, this type of analysis is suggestive of the relational context we have been discussing since it not only appeals to the individual, but to the individual in relation.

The psychology of Erikson and the adaptive-evolutionary analyses of aging presented here suggest, albeit in different ways and to different ends, that a relational value is central in aging. More than this even, both of these perspectives lend some support, at the level of the underlying interpretation of basic human needs and developmental processes, to the claim of the historic theological literature that the moral praxis of aging ought to be conceived in such a way as to lead to the enhancing and enriching of the lives of others.

PASTORAL CARE SITUATIONS

Betty Carlton is a 73-year-old lawyer who heads a local chapter of a national organization for the aged. She lives with her housekeeper in a sprawling house in a wealthy section of a large metropolitan city. She says she has not undergone any major changes recently, except for a minor hearing problem. While she no longer practices law, she is a frequent lobbyist in the state legislature, though she is beginning to look forward to moving to a warmer climate.

Jack Jackson is a 68-year-old man. A resident of a county home for the aged, he is frequently depressed and occasionally refuses to bathe or feed himself. He rarely speaks and suffers from a variety of physical ailments. His wife died several years previously. Jack believes he has several children, but is unable to recall their names or where they live.

Frank and Janice Stanger have been married for fifty-two years. She is eighty years of age, he is eighty-two. The Stangers live next door to their daughter and her family and are often asked to take care of their grandchildren—"A little more often than I would like," Janice says. They attend church regularly and occasionally visit with longtime friends, though they find themselves desiring to spend more of their time alone now. Frank is worried about his wife and fears what will happen if she dies first.

Old age is the witness of a life. More than the historic theological literature would have granted, it is a witness that encompasses the essential ambiguities of life: a witness in which the joys and sorrows, triumphs and defeats, tragedies and ironies of life remain in that essential tension found in those of all ages. Old age deserves neither our romanticizing nor our scorn, for it partakes of the same stuff of which all of life is made. But we must recognize that, as with the witness of all life, it is given to others as well as to self. This insight of the historic theological literature on aging (and of some contemporary interpretations of the experience of aging) forms an important dimension of pastoral care with older adults. Pastoral care asks not only whether the witness of the lives of Betty Carlton, Jack Jackson, and Frank and Janice Stanger is a witness of happiness and satisfaction. It must also ask whether the witness of each one is enhancing of life itself, whether their old age witnesses—within its ambiguities—to a meaningful horizon of the moral becoming of others, whether it finally affirms, in Erikson's words, a "life-giving self."

The moral praxis of aging envisioned here represents neither a capitulation to self or others, neither a capitulation to exclusive self-regard or exclusive other-regard, but rather a mutuality (though not necessarily a complementarity) of what is good-for-self and what is good-for-others. Neither George and Betty Anderson nor Margaret Arnold is called here to disavow the reality of their own needs for the sake of others. Janice Stanger is not called to take care of her grandchildren whenever her daughter wishes her to do so. The issue is more subtle than this. Older adults are called to forms of relationships in which their own fulfillment expresses care for the fulfillment of others. To put this in the terms of the previous chapter, a relational resolution of the metaethical task transcends the individual older adult in its provision of a meaningful horizon to the moral becoming of others. But individual life in old age is itself made possible by such transcendence—providing the certainty of its own meaningfulness (i.e., its own integrity) in past, present, and future.

It is obviously often a vital step in pastoral care to help older adults feel good about themselves, although we insist that the guiding vision of pastoral care with the aging cannot stop there. The church's witness with regard to aging, which pastoral care re-presents in concrete situations and under particular existential and cultural conditions, extends to love of those others whose lives form a part of one's own and that one Other who calls us forward in love.

The forms such expressions of care take in older adulthood may change somewhat given the shift in emphasis from moral becoming proper to the meaning of one's moral becoming as the focal intentionality of the aging self. We need not read this, as Bertram Cohler does, as a decreased desire to care for others, but rather as a change in the forms of expression of such care in the context of the metaethical task. Even such things as meditation and reminiscence, as Erikson and the historic theological literature suggest, may contribute to the lives of others by providing a vision of a meaningful heritage and a meaningful end to life. They provide, if you will, a meaningful horizon to the moral becoming of others.[23]

Older adults come to the metaethical task with their own particular developmental histories, of course. The way in which they will seek to deal with its challenges will vary depending upon their object-relations development, their moral and faith development, their ego development, etc. In seeking to enable older adults to affirm their life-giving selves, therefore, pastoral care must be developmentally appropriate both in its expectations and in its concrete applications. We must allow, in other words, that the individual forms of expressing a relational resolution of the metaethical task will vary. We cannot apply the relational interpretation of the moral praxis of aging irrespective of the particularities of the way of life of the individual before us. And, indeed, pastoral care with the aging will frequently entail the complicated task of helping older adults sort out conflicts that arise between the values of good-for-self and good-for-others within that developmental diversity. Yet the underlying vision here is that *pastoral care with the aging involves enabling older adults meaningfully and appropriately to care for and contribute to the lives of others even as it enables older adults meaningfully and appropriately to care for themselves.*

It is surely clear, however (for the reasons cited in the previous chapter), that pastoral care with the aging cannot simply work with older adults in this regard. The community itself must encourage and sustain the care and contribution of older adults, lest that care become trivialized. The community itself must come to understand that its own life is enriched and enhanced by the particular forms of care the relational resolution of the metaethical task evinces and that the demands of care *for* older adults necessitates such a vision. A variety of programs, if developed out of (or lead to renewal in or transformation of) the church's or community's normative vision, would enable this task: Friendly Visiting, Foster Grandparents, Heritage Centers, Prayer Ministries, etc.[24] Such programs, however, cannot be bandaids or bones thrown in the direction of a neglected need. Rather, the value-consensus of the church and community itself must be challenged and formed in such a way that these or similar programs are expressions of the requirements of love (both of self and others). Thus, part of the task of *pastoral care with older adults involves facilitating the building of a value-consensus within the community which encourages and sustains older adults' affirming of their life-giving selves.*

THE MORAL PRAXIS OF AGING AND
THE PROBLEM OF HOPE

For some in our time, the relational ground of the moral praxis of aging is an answer to the problem of hope suggested in the last chapter: the consummation of hope in old age is made possible through the contributions older adults can make to the lives of others. Hope in old age is found, it is said, in envisioning the positive benefits one's life can make to future generations. But surely a problem is likely to strike us here. It is a problem captured by a 69-year-old woman who had been confined to her bed after suffering a stroke. Her minister invited her to participate in the ministry of the church by writing the birthday greeting cards the church sent to its members. She was elated at being asked and for several months her spirits lifted as she carefully carried out the task. One day when her minister was visiting, however, she seemed distant and saddened. When asked what was troubling her, she replied: "I'm not sure about those birthday cards anymore. I'm here with my nurse and I'm so alone sometimes. It just doesn't seem like much for a person to do. It's just not much of a life, is it?" The relational resolution of the metaethical task suggests that fulfillment in old age hinges, in part, on the ways in which our lives enrich those of others. But the realities confronted by those older adults suffering from debilitating illness or poverty ought to give us pause in this regard. The range of possibility for hope *in this sense* may seem severely limited.

We need not retreat to the "hard cases," however, to note the profound depths of this problem. In its deepest sense, it is true for all. As Schubert Ogden has written:

> If the only contributions our lives could make were the contributions they make to other creaturely lives as limited as our own, they would make no abiding difference and, in that sense, would be meaningless. Death and transience—the perpetual perishing of all things in the

ever-rolling stream of time—would be the last word about each of us, and about all of us together.[25]

We are led again to the problem of hope as a limiting dimension of human existence. What, then, are we to make of the hope of old age if, finally, neither its psychological nor its ethical dimensions can sufficiently ground it?

CHAPTER 7

Hope, Blessing,
and
Redemption

This book, as I have said, is an effort to compose a way of life: to develop an interpretation of human fulfillment in aging with the intention of clarifying certain foundational issues in pastoral care with older adults. To this point we have dealt with three issues: (1) how we are to conceptualize certain foundational questions concerning human nature and human development in aging, (2) how, within this understanding, we might conceptualize the intentionality of the aging self, and (3) how we are to conceive the moral praxis of aging. The constructive character of the argument looks like this: I have proposed a dialectically progressive reading of growth with aging through the idea of the metaethical task of old age and have suggested that the practical-moral thrust of such an understanding is best articulated in a relational manner.

THE AESTHETIC CONTEXT OF AGING

There is, however, at least one question that remains to be addressed at this point: What kind of a world is it within which all of this makes sense? This question may be seen to arise directly out of the discussion of the last two chapters: How are we to understand the ultimate context of the world of an aging self for whom *this* moral praxis exists as a meaningful and coherent possibility (as self not, finally, self-contradicted)? This no doubt sounds rather abstract at this point. But I suspect the question here only sounds so abstract because it is so formatively interior to our reflection and action.

Frankly, in our day-to-day lives, and even in our pastoral care, we are not apt to give much thought to such a question. Yet, our actions in this day-to-day world inevitably reveal certain understandings of what we think the ultimate context of our world is like. Our sense of its coldness and warmth, responsiveness and unresponsiveness, fullness and emptiness, indifference and caring (in essence, its beauty and ugliness) forms that horizon of experience within which we live our everyday lives. We experience this horizon as both exterior to the self (as "the way reality finally is") and as interior to the self (as the telotic core of selfhood: as "who I most fundamentally am" and "who I most fundamentally am called to be").

Our own particular sense of this horizon of experience is disclosed in those foundational images and metaphors that lie within our most basic ways of making our experience meaningful. In this sense, we might say that images and metaphors form the aesthetic context of our experience and reflection in that they are the means by which, in Robert Neville's phrase, "imagination synthesizes its components into experience."[1] Our reflection on this horizon of experience as it relates to older adulthood, then, may be seen to have to do with the aesthetic context of aging. In this chapter, therefore, we are seeking to reflect critically not directly on the action of older adults in the world, but on the "form of the world" within which such action takes place.[2]

Think, for example, about this comment of William Clements in his discussion of problems that can arise in the failure to recognize the creative potential of aging:

> Where the growthful possibilities in old age are not seen the result is a state of entropy—a gradual running down of the organism because energizing creativity is lacking. Entropy increases as expectations for novelty and meaningful directivity diminish. You may have heard older people speak of the difficulties of living "with nothing to look forward to." Imagine for a moment what your life might be like if suddenly you found yourself without a single goal you thought worthy of pursuit.[3]

What Clements is doing here is using the metaphor of entropy to reflect on the way some older adults experience the horizon of aging. In this perspective, the aesthetic context of human action for the aging self is understood metaphorically within the terms of the entropic process: our lives simply decline into that random meaninglessness that characterizes the final nature of things.

Think also of the way in which Rev. Williams reflected on his interaction with George and Betty Anderson. The metaphor of sabbath was the way Rev. Williams sought to make sense of the horizon of the experience of aging. Aging here was placed in the context of fulfilling the role God has ordained for the final phase of life: enjoyment and rest from one's previous labors.

In our effort to think critically about the nature of human fulfillment in aging, then, we must forthrightly take responsibility for our fundamental images and metaphors (for our sense of the aesthetic context of aging) and seek to determine to what extent they are adequate and meaningful. We cannot deal with the broader dimensions of this problem in this space. Nonetheless, we can begin to approach this issue by working with the problem of hope.

In the previous chapter we have seen the problem of hope arise in two ways. It arose first in our discussion of the metaethical task of aging. I suggested there that an affirmation of the hope- and trust-infusing foundations of existence was entailed by the very idea of the metaethical task. Yet, are the foundations of our existence indeed confirming of the possibility of the realization of value in later adulthood? Is it possible to affirm this without romanticizing the losses and declining abilities that accompany our later years? But the problem of hope arose in another way as well. The relational resolution of the metaethical task, I noted, is threatened with final meaninglessness and our hope with trivialization if in Schubert Ogden's words, "the only contribution our lives could make were the contributions they make to other creaturely lives as limited as our own."[4] How, then, are we to understand the aesthetic context of the world of an aging self for whom *this* moral praxis and *this* intentionality exist as meaningful and coherent possibilities? How are we to "account for the hope that is in us?" In order to approach these two dimensions of the problem of hope I will initially turn to the discussion of blessing, for I believe it provides us the beginnings of an answer.

THE BLESSING OF AGE

The image of the blessing of age was prominent in certain of the historic theological interpretations of the aesthetic context of aging. Yet, the idea that old age is a blessing of God may well strike us today as anachronistic at best and cruelly paradoxical at worst. Such an image may have more easily made sense in those premodern cultures where at least the official ideology was gerontocratic. In many preliterate folk cultures, ancient Greek and Roman societies, and even in Puritan America, the idea of old age as a blessing may have been relatively more consistent with certain aspects of the community's self-understanding (even if not its actual practice). In a time in which the signs of aging are to be hidden if they cannot be fixed, however, the blessing of age is rapidly reduced to its potential for leisure and consumption. There are at least four problems that make the recovery of the idea of the blessing of age difficult today: (1) the various conditions of old age, (2) the trivialization of age, (3) the ideological components of the idea, and (4) its classical theistic underpinnings in the historic theological literature. Each of these deserves a brief comment.

First, it is difficult to understand what kind of a blessing it could be to be old and ill or old and poor in our time. Where is the blessing, we are likely to ask, for the elderly woman suffering from Alzheimer's disease? Where is the blessing, we ought also to ask, for the destitute aged of our great cities? Cotton Mather wrote that "Old age ought always to be as a box of ointment, perfuming and refreshing standersby as often as it opens."[5] Within such an image of old age, the idea of old age as a blessing would be easily connected with notions of cultural civility. Yet, we cannot insulate our understanding of aging from the harder realities of the aging self simply to save the notion of blessing. We must frankly admit that in our time the notion of old age as a blessing of God tends to smack of that romantic consolation of what Johann Baptist Metz calls middle-class religion.[6]

Second, the trivialization of age in our day tends to undercut the perception of the aged as possessing special attributes or qualities that could sustain the idea of the blessing of age despite loss and decline. This problem is exemplified in Erik Erikson's recent reflections on his own understanding of old age; an understanding, as we have seen, that makes use of terms like "integrity" and "wisdom." As Erikson has reflected on the changes that have occurred between the time of his first formulation of the theory and the present:

> The predominant image of old age was then altogether different. One could still think in terms of "elders," the few wise men and women who quietly lived up to their stage-appropriate assignment and knew how to

die with some dignity in cultures where long survival appeared to be a divine gift to and a special obligation for a few. But do such terms still hold when old age is represented by a quite numerous, fast-increasing, and reasonably well-preserved group of "elderlies"?[7]

Erikson, of course, has not abandoned his interpretation of old age and, indeed, there seem good reasons to maintain it in terms of its understanding of certain of the psychological dynamics of aging and his understanding of the moral praxis of aging. Yet, the general problem here does call into question the understanding of the broader horizons within which that interpretation (and, indeed, that of the historic theological literature in some respects) functioned.

A third difficulty with recovering the idea of the blessing of age has to do with certain ideological uses to which it was put and the social structure which it rationalized. The notion of old age as a blessing of God was, at least in certain contexts, a court of appeal in the justification of patriarchal gerontocracy. Domination usually receives some cultural rationalization and the idea of the blessing of age was certainly a readily available one. Some historians have even suggested that the decline in status of the elderly in the contemporary world has its roots in the Enlightenment rejection of traditional authority (as this applies to gerontocracy, of course, and not necessarily to patriarchy).[8] If the idea of the blessing of age has no other practical outcome than the domination of women and the younger generations, it is an idea well lost.

Finally, fourth, given the classical theistic notions that undergirded it, the idea of old age as a blessing of God tended to be in some tension with the fact that not all aged persons had lived, or were living, particularly praiseworthy lives. We have discussed this problem in chapter 2 and I will return to it shortly.

Given these difficulties, as well as those other tensions that arose in the tradition itself on this point, it may seem best simply to abandon the idea altogether. Yet I think there are good reasons to seek to reconceptualize a certain aspect of what underlay the idea of the blessing of age. In doing so we will find one possible response of the Christian community to the problem of hope in old age. In order to suggest why I think this is the case, it will be helpful to turn initially to Claus Westermann's discussion of blessing in the biblical materials.

THE IDEA OF BLESSING

Blessing, as Westermann says, tended to refer to God's action with respect to the provision of the possibility of growth and maturation. In other words, the idea of blessing refers not to God's salvific action and human response, but to the continuities of life: God's presence in the cycle of generations. As he writes, "It is God's blessing that lets the child grow into a man or woman, that bestows such manifold talents, and that provides physical and spiritual food from so many sources."[9]

In its early history in the biblical materials, the idea of blessing was unconditional: once a blessing was bestowed it could not be withdrawn. At a later stage of development, however, blessing came to be seen as conditional. In Deut. 7:12–13, for example, the idea of God's blessing was incorporated into the covenant and was conditional upon the obedience of the people. Thus, blessing was subject to the limitations of the curse—the result of the people's disobedience. With the destruction of the temple, however, the idea of blessing came to be seen more in relation to individual obedience rather than the obedience of the people. As the book of Job and various psalms make clear, however, this association of obedience and blessing came under increasing tension as it was recognized that even individual obedience did not necessarily guarantee good fortune.

In the New Testament, the concept of blessing underwent a partial Christianization. In Westermann's words, "Christ himself becomes the one who blesses, and all of God's bestowal of blessing became connected with God's work in Christ."[10] Yet, as he observes, there are really two concepts of blessing in the New Testament: one which clearly suggests the Christianization of blessing and one which carries forward the traditional conception. The persistence of the older way of construing blessing suggests that the Christian witness regarding salvation and justification did not eclipse the concern with God's empowering presence in the continuities of life in the here and now—in, if you will, the cycle of generations.

It is instructive to note, I think, that the historic theological understanding of old age as a blessing echoes many of the tensions and transformations suggested in the biblical materials themselves: the question of whether the blessing of age was conditional or unconditional, the question of whether the idea of the blessing of age was simply to be subsumed by God's saving act in Christ, and how—if the blessing of age was unconditional—moral and religious responsibility could still be made coherent. The two most frequent approaches, as I have said, either spiritualized the concept of old age or made the blessing of age conditional on appropriate response to the reconciliation wrought by Christ. Neither of these, however, seems a particularly appealing prospect: the first because it removes the question from the material contexts of our lives, the second because it raises again—albeit now in Christianized form—the problems of connecting the *granting* of God's blessing to obedience in matters of growth, maturation, and decline.

Despite these difficulties, the idea of blessing does seem to be getting an important point: God's action and human response must be seen not only "in the event of deliverance, the proclamation of the message and its acceptance by faith, saying yes or no to God in confession, the pronouncement of forgiveness and justification," but also in "growth and maturation, prospering and succeeding, expanding and contracting, taking root and spreading out."[11] It is through God's action of blessing, in other words, that the realization of value in the mundane and everyday occurrences of our lives and in those continuities that underlie the cycle of generations is made possible. The question here is, given the difficulties with the idea of the blessing of age we have noted, is there any way meaningfully to recapture theologically this dimension of God's action as it relates to aging?

TOWARD A RECONCEPTUALIZATION
OF BLESSING

God's actions of blessing are but one dimension of the way in which Christians have sought to describe the horizon of human experience. It is a way in which the horizons of our experience of the cycle of generations and the continuities of our lives are made meaningful: the values that we realize in our everyday lives are enabled by God's actions of blessing.[12] To speak of the blessing of age, therefore, may seem to mean that there is a *characteristic value* that may be realized in later adulthood (which is obviously not to say it is the only value realized in later adulthood). Our previous discussion suggests that value might be this: older adults may provide a meaningful horizon to the moral becoming of others and, in so doing, find their own integrity in working through the metaethical task. The blessing of age, then, is the relational value that may be realized in the appropriate resolution of the metaethical task.

Herein lies one response to the problem of hope in aging, for God's blessing is understood as God's envisioning of a potential for the realization of the greatest value for each moment and condition of our lives. God's granting of blessing, in this sense, is unconditional: within each moment and condition God's blessing is present. The moment or condition *itself* is not God's blessing, but rather God blesses us in each moment and condition by offering us the possibility of the creation of value. While God's blessing is unconditional, however, the actual realization of value in our lives requires our action. The fruit of God's blessing may be realized or not, may be actively thwarted by us or be but partially realized in our brokenness. Our realizing the fruits of God's blessing in our lives is not the sole action of God, but the cocreating of God and the world.

Two points about this reconceptualization need to be highlighted. First, the blessing of age here is understood as unconditional in the sense that God's actions of blessing are not withheld in the face of human brokenness or sin. Such a view seems consistent with the Christian witness. In the Christ-event, we witness to the *universal* love and forgiveness of God. Westermann notes that, in the New Testament, the connection between blessing and curse is broken in the work of Christ.[13] One need not (and ought not), interpret this situation with the supercessionist overtones implied in Westermann's discussion, however, to note the central point: blessing is an aspect of God's "pure, unbounded love." Yet, as I have noted, while God's granting of blessing is unconditional, our realization of the fruits of God's blessing is hardly guaranteed. God's blessing is not a magic formula uttered from above that guarantees our good fortune. We must recognize, with the process theologians, that God does not (cannot) solely determine the outcome of events in the world. God's activity is more that of persuasion (or luring toward the realization of value) than that of compulsion or coercion. Humans have real freedom and, to use William James's apt phrase, God is "but one helper, *primus inter pares,* in the midst of all the shapers of the great world's fate."[14] Real human freedom, of course, carries with it real human responsibility. In a world not guaranteed of the emergence of the good by divine fiat, there is the threat of real evil and the consequent necessity of human action toward the realization of the good in our world and in our lives. In more traditional language, God's will is not so much enacted onto recalcitrant history as it is a persuasive force that may yet be modified, thwarted, or positively embodied in our own becoming and the becoming of our world. God's blessing is unconditional, but our realization of the fruits of God's blessing is not. The blessing of age, therefore, is offered by God to each older adult, but its actualization depends on their response to that blessing.

Second, to speak of the blessing of age is not to say that we must see the various conditions that may afflict those in older adulthood as good or, worse, as God's "reward" or (if we think God's blessing is absent) God's "punishment" of us. God's blessing does not refer to God's envisioning a potential in the best of all possible worlds (which is the way many of us are likely to understand it), but rather to God's envisioning a potential in our real world and our present circumstances within it. To speak of the blessing of age, therefore, is not to say that old age is devoid of hardship, loss, or disease. *Rather, it is to say that God provides a potential for the realization of the greatest value even in these circumstances.* The idea of the blessing of age here does not require us to romanticize hardship, loss, or disease. There are, as many older adults know only too well, in James's phrase, "real losses." But loss is not all there is even though sometimes it is all we can see. God suffers with us in our hardship, loss, or disease, and offers us blessing. God suffers with the victim of Alzheimer's disease, with the destitute aged of our great cities, with Margaret Arnold and Jack Jackson. God experiences the pain of an aging self struggling to maintain its coherence. God suffers with us and offers us blessing— the power of life in the face of death. God suffers with us and offers us the power of a life-giving self.

BLESSING AND REDEMPTION

This understanding of the blessing of age provides, I believe, one response to the problem of hope in aging. The aesthetic context of aging is here seen as hope-full and trust-full in its disclosure of a divine presence with us that confirms and sustains the possibility of realizing values in old age. To speak of God's blessing, in other words, is to say that there is an ontological ground to our hope. Yet to say this may simply seem to highlight the second problem of hope in aging: the final meaningfulness of the values realized in later adulthood.

The idea of the blessing of age is not fully adequate as a means of disclosing the horizons of the experience of aging (nor is it a sufficient response to the problem of hope). This was clearly realized in the historic theological literature itself. Discussions of redemption, salvation, and eternal life were ever-present counterpoints to the discussion of blessing. Yet the classical understanding of God that undergirded much of this discussion created difficult problems: with God conceived, in many instances, as entirely self-sufficient and unaffected by the world in any essential manner, how is one to make sense of the idea of the religioethical witness of age? As Charles Hartshorne has written in a broader context: "You cannot be motivated by consideration of the value you contribute to another, if that other is so constituted so that he can receive no value from any source."[15] To refer back to Erikson's language, then, the need of the older adult for that "mysterious, that ultimate Other" is not only the need for One who gives the gift of existence, but also for that Other who lovingly responds to (and thereby is changed by) the "I" who acts. The need is not only for the existence of the Other, but that the Other exists in relation and in some way saves in their being, by virtue of that relation, the value realized by the "I" who acts. Again with the process theologians, I think we must say that God is affected by the world. Indeed, God's redemptive action—as decisively disclosed by Jesus—is predicated on that very fact.

In Jesus, God's actions of blessing and redemption are disclosed as integrally related. Through God's redemptive action, the realization of value in our lives is saved from final meaninglessness. In God's redemptive action, God "creatively synthesizes all other things into his own actual being as God."[16] God takes in the value realized in the world, weaves it into Godself, and thus preserves it everlastingly— even to the extent of its contributing to the ongoing blessing of God in our lives and the becoming of our world. It is because God redeems our lives from final meaninglessness that the blessing of age carries the force that it does: the question of the meaningfulness of one's moral becoming, and its potential relational resolution, occur in a world where God confirms the seriousness of this venture of the aging self, even as the relational resolution of the metaethical task confirms, mediately, the seriousness of the venture of moral becoming for the younger generations.

PASTORAL CARE AND THE
BLESSING OF AGE

A young woman seminarian was working part time in a nursing home for the aged. In discussing her experience at one point, she said: "Old people are so cute. They're wonderful really, you know. Oh, sometimes they have problems and things, but they have lived so long and everything. God has really blessed them." The idea of the blessing of age is not an excuse for naiveté, immaturity, or fantasy in our pastoral care with older adults. Indeed, it is not an *excuse* for anything. It is a dimension of that interpretive lens those engaged in pastoral care with older adults must bring to the real world of aging, not the world of dime novels or B movies where loss and suffering are but illusions by the end of the last chapter or final reel. The idea of the blessing of age stands in sharp contrast to such distortion: it acknowledges a God who suffers with us in our losses and struggles and offers us blessing.

But the idea of the blessing of age also stands in contrast to images of simple loss and decline. As Gordon Jackson has written concerning older adults in nursing homes:

> Hope is in a God who has not forgotten these. . . . God's caring is seen here not in a theological *tour de force* in which God can do everything, but for some reason, known only to God, won't. In the view of process theology God cannot do everything. Yet, there is a Caring that struggles with a body that has outlasted its mind, perhaps to provide as much lure as that enfeebled organism can respond to. There is a certain beauty in the struggle that God and each organism are engaged in to give even a limited sense of life to each experiencing moment within a nursing home.[17]

God's blessing arises in multitudinous ways in older adulthood, depending upon physical and cognitive abilities, emotional, moral, and faith development, sociocultural circumstances, etc. The way isolated in this essay, in speaking of the blessing of age, is God's provision of a possibility for actualizing a relational value in response to the metaethical task. But whatever the circumstances of older adults, the idea of blessing allows us to restate what process philosophy finds in the very nature of reality: a divine lure toward the creation of value.

Pastoral care with the aging, then, involves enabling older adults to understand God's presence with them as One who blesses and One who redeems. This task of pastoral care may or may not be carried out in explicitly Christian or even religious terms with some older adults. In our caring for some older adults the task may simply be our enabling (or "luring") of their experiencing of the seriousness and meaningfulness of their efforts to actualize certain values, meet certain needs, etc. It may simply involve our confirmation of the seriousness of their struggle to affirm their life-giving selves in the context of their aging. It may simply involve our suggesting developmentally appropriate avenues potentially available to them to contribute to the lives of others and to the enhancing of their own lives. God's working occurs whether we mention God or not. For others, of course, more explicit references to God's working will be appropriate. Whatever one's stance on this issue, the task of pastoral care with the aging is to affirm and facilitate the actualization of God's blessing in older adulthood. In this we oursleves must be aware, and perhaps acknowledge to them, that yes, our life is different and is being enriched in various ways for their being a part of it. In this we witness not only to our presence with them and the meaning of their presence with us, but to the One whose blessing and redeeming grounds our mutual care.

Pastoral care with the aging involves the building of a value-consensus within the community which affirms in word and deed God's presence with us throughout our lives as One who blesses and One who redeems. As the historic theological literature on aging suggested, human fulfillment in old age hinges on an understanding of community and social interchange in which the emotional, moral, and religious interconnection of the generations is firmly acknowledged. In affirming God's work of blessing and redeeming, we acknowledge God's empowering presence and loving care for all in "birth and maturity. . . . the union of man and woman and the birth of children . . . aging and death."[18] We are "a people" despite our vast differences because God's blessing and redeeming are universal, not fettered by bonds of age or class or color or religion. We are covenanted, bound to each other and to God. Human fulfillment in aging and, indeed, the fulfillment of those of all generations depends upon our seeking to make this truth, this promise, a reality in life.

Notes

CHAPTER 1

1. The phrase "mental hypochondriasis" is from Jerome Frank, *Persuasion and Healing*, rev. ed. (New York: Schocken Books, 1973), 12. The classic work on "psychological man" is Philip Rieff's *The Triumph of the Therapeutic* (New York: Harper & Row, 1966).

2. It is popular today to differentiate the terms "aging" and "the aged." This reflects important concerns. Nonetheless, in this essay I will use the term "aging" to refer to later adulthood. It has the benefit of suggesting that older adulthood is a process and not simply a state of being ("aged"), and is less cumbersome than some alternatives.

3. Thomas C. Oden, *Care of Souls in the Classic Tradition* (Philadelphia: Fortress Press, 1984).

4. Don S. Browning, *Religious Ethics and Pastoral Care* (Philadelphia: Fortress Press, 1983), 122.

CHAPTER 2

1. The figures here are from U.S. Bureau of the Census, America in Transition: An Aging Society, *Current population reports*, ser. p–23, no. 128 (Washington, D.C.: U.S. Government Printing Office, 1983). Carl Eisdorfer's remark is from his "Conceptual Models of Aging," *American Psychologist* (February 1983): 197.

2. Paul G. Glick, "Updating the Life Cycle of the Family," *Journal of Marriage and the Family* 39 (February 1977): 9.

3. David Hackett Fischer, *Growing Old in America*, expanded ed. (New York: Oxford University Press, 1978), 4.

4. Robert Kastenbaum, "Exist and Existence," in *Aging, Death, and the Completion of Being*, ed. David D. Van Tassel (Philadelphia: University of Pennsylvania Press, 1979), 77.

5. Andrew Achenbaum, *Old Age in the New Land* (Baltimore: Johns Hopkins University Press, 1978), 4.

6. Leo Tolstoy, *The Cossacks and Other Stories,* trans. Rosemary Edmonds (Harmondsworth, Eng.: Penguin Books, 1960), 137.

7. Robert Kastenbaum, "Gerontology's Search for Understanding," *The Gerontologist* 18 (September 1978): 60–61. Recent efforts to address certain of these questions may be found in three collections of essays: Patrick L. McKee, ed., *Philosophical Foundations of Gerontology* (New York: Human Sciences Press, 1982); Stuart F. Spicker, Kathleen M. Woodword, and David D. Van Tassel, eds., *Aging and the Elderly: Humanistic Perspectives in Gerontology* (Atlantic Highlands, N.J.: Humanities Press, 1978); and Van Tassel, ed., *Aging, Death, and the Completion of Being.* From the perspective of the Christian theological tradition, see the essays in William M. Clements, ed., *Ministry with the Aging: Designs-Challenges-Foundations* (San Francisco: Harper & Row, 1981).

8. In an otherwise helpful discussion of therapeutic techniques, this problem is illustrated in the discussion of Martha Storandt, *Counseling and Therapy with Older Adults* (Boston: Little, Brown & Co., 1983).

9. See, for example, Richard Bernstein, *Beyond Objectivism and Relativism* (Philadelphia: University of Pennsylvania Press, 1983).

10. See, for example, Andrew Achenbaum, *Shades of Gray: Old Age, American Values, and Federal Policies Since 1920* (Boston: Little, Brown & Co., 1982).

11. Gerald Gruman, "Cultural Origins of Present-day 'Age-ism,'" in *Aging and the Elderly,* ed. Spicker et al., 359–87.

12. David Stannard, "Growing Up and Growing Old," in *Aging and the Elderly,* ed. Spicker et al., 9–20.

13. A variety of issues related in this point are discussed in Michael J. Sandel, *Liberalism and the Limits of Justice* (New York and Cambridge: Cambridge University Press, 1982).

CHAPTER 3

1. Oden, *Care of Souls in the Classic Tradition.*

2. Martin J. Heinecken and Ralph R. Hellerich, *The Church's Ministry with Older Adults: A Theological Basis* (New York: Lutheran Church in America, 1976), 1.

3. Martin J. Heinecken, "Christian Theology and Aging: Basic Affirmations," in *Ministry with the Aging,* ed. Clements, 76.

4. Christopher Lasch, *The Culture of Narcissism* (New York: W. W. Norton, 1979). See also Jaroslav Pelikan, *The Vindication of Tradition* (New Haven: Yale University Press, 1984).

5. William Bridge, "A Word to the Aged," in *The Works of William Bridge* (London: Thomas Tegg, 1845), 184.

6. St. Ambrose, *Complete Letters,* trans. Sister Mary Melchior Beyenka, vol. 26 of The Fathers of the Church (Washington, D.C.: Catholic University of America Press, 1973), 40.

7. Cotton Mather, *The Old Man's Honour, or, The Hoary Head Found in the*

Way of Righteousness (Boston, 1690), 28–29.

8. John Calvin, *Commentaries*, trans. Charles Bingham, 44 vols. (Edinburgh: Calvin Translation Society, 1845), 5:19.

9. Ibid.

10. Calvin, *Institutes of the Christian Religion*, ed. John T. McNeill (Philadelphia: Westminster Press, 1960), 403.

11. Calvin, *Commentaries*, 44:129.

12. Ibid.

13. Ibid., 16:400–401. For a discussion of the transformation of the Calvinist association of sin with old age in New England Puritanism, see Thomas Cole, "The 'Enlightened' View of Aging: Victorian Morality in a New Key," *The Hastings Center Report* (June 1983): 34–40.

14. Calvin, *Institutes*, 686.

15. Ibid., 688.

16. Calvin, *Commentaries*, 41:283.

17. Ibid.

18. Calvin, *Institutes*, 702.

19. Ibid., 703.

20. Wilhelm Niesel, *The Theology of Calvin* (Grand Rapids: Baker Book House, 1980), 146.

21. Calvin, *Institutes*, 712–13.

22. Ibid., 713.

23. Calvin, *Commentaries*, 10:504.

24. Ibid.

25. Ibid., 505.

26. Keith Thomas, "Age and Authority in Early Modern England," *Proceedings of the British Academy* 62 (1976): 244.

27. Calvin, *Commentaries*, 2:37.

28. Ibid.

29. Ibid.

30. *Augustine: Earlier Writings*, ed. J. H. S. Burleigh, vol. 6 of Library of Christian Classics (Philadelphia: Westminster Press, 1953), 249.

31. Ibid.

32. Augustine, *Sermons on the Liturgical Seasons*, trans. Sister Mary Muldowney, vol. 38 of the Fathers of the Church (Washington, D.C.: Catholic University of America Press, 1959), 158.

33. Ambrose, *Letters*, 69.

34. Jerome, *Letters and Select Works*, vol. 6 of Nicene and Post-Nicene Fathers, 2d ser., ed. Philip Schaff and Henry Wace (Grand Rapids: Wm. B. Eerdmans, 1972), 90.

35. Friedrich Schleiermacher, *Soliloquies* (Chicago: Open Court Publishing, 1926), 94.

36. Jerome, *Letters and Select Works*, 90.

37. Theodore Parker, "The Aged," in *Social Classes in a Republic* (Boston: American Unitarian Associates, n.d.), 185–86.

38. St. Chrysostom, *Homilies on Hebrews*, vol. 14 of Nicene and Post-Nicene Fathers, 401.

39. Ibid.

40. Ibid., 498.

41. Ibid., 401.

42. Ibid.

43. Bridge, "A Word to the Aged," 189.

44. Mather, *The Old Man's Honour*, 33.

45. Chrysostom, *Homilies on Hebrews*, 402.

46. Ambrose, *Letters*, 69.

47. Bridge, "A Word to the Aged," 186.

48. Clement of Alexandria, "The Instructor," in *Writings of Clement of Alexandria*, trans. William Wilson, Ante-Nicene Christian Library (Edinburgh, 1872), 319.

49. Mather, *The Old Man's Honour*, 35, 36.

50. *The Practical Works of the Rev. Richard Baxter*, ed. William Orme, 20 vols. (London: James Duncan, 1830), 4:396.

51. Ibid., 397.

52. Ibid., 398.

53. Ibid.

54. Ibid., 399.

55. Ibid., 398.

56. Ibid., 399.

57. Ibid.

58. Ibid., 15:392.

59. Ibid.

60. Ibid., 392–93.

61. Thomas, "Age and Authority in Early Modern England," 210.

62. Ibid.

63. *Practical Works of Richard Baxter*, 4:402.

CHAPTER 4

1. Bridge, "A Word to the Aged," 181.

2. Ibid.

3. David Gutmann, "Psychoanalysis and Aging: A Developmental Perspective," in *The Course of Life*, ed. Stanley Greenspan and Sidney Pollock, 3 vols. (Washington, D.C.: National Institutes of Mental Health, 1980), 3:489. See also Paul Pruyser, "Aging: Upward, Downward, or Forward?" in *Toward a Theology of Aging*, ed. Seward Hiltner (New York: Human Sciences Press, 1975), and Lawrence Lazarus, ed., *Clinical Approaches to Psychotherapy with the Elderly* (Washington, D.C.: American Psychiatric Press, 1984).

4. David Kelsey, "Human Being," in *Christian Theology*, ed. Peter Hodgson and Robert King (Philadelphia: Fortress Press, 1982), 148.

5. Schleiermacher, *Soliloquies*, 92.

6. Mary Midgley, *Beast and Man: The Roots of Human Nature* (Ithaca, N.Y.: Cornell University Press, 1978), xiii.

7. Schubert Ogden, *Faith and Freedom* (Nashville: Abingdon Press, 1979), 68.

8. To say that the "high" in humans is natural and historical does not mean that we must necessarily interpret it mechanistically or collapse all notions of transcendence. The problem here is as much with the interpretation of "nature" as anything else.

9. Claus Westermann, *Creation* (Philadelphia: Fortress Press, 1974), 78. See also the interesting discussion in Lynn A. de Silva, *The Problem of the Self in Buddhism and Christianity* (New York: Barnes & Noble, 1978).

10. See Leslie Fiedler, "Eros and Thanatos: Old Age in Love," in *Aging, Death, and the Completion of Being,* ed. Van Tassel, 235–54.

11. For a discussion of Metchnikoff's position, see Achenbaum, *Old Age in the New Land,* 44–45.

12. George Sacher, "Longevity, Aging, and Death: An Evolutionary Perspective," *The Gerontologist* 18 (February 1978): 118.

13. Morton Lieberman and Sheldon Tobin, *The Experience of Old Age* (New York: Basic Books, 1983), 241.

14. The classic text here is Elaine Cummings and William Henry, *Growing Old* (New York: Basic Books, 1961).

15. Erdman Palmore, *The Honorable Elders* (Durham, N.C.: Duke University Press, 1975), 5.

16. The critical literature is immense. I would, however, especially note Arlie Russel Hochschild, "Disengagement Theory: A Critique and Proposal," *American Sociological Review* 40 (October 1975): 553–69.

17. See, for an early example, C. Eisdorfer and M. P. Lawton, eds., *The Psychology of Adult Development and Aging* (Washington, D.C.: American Psychological Association, 1973).

18. Paul B. Baltes and K. Warner Schaie, "Aging and IQ: The Myth of the Twilight Years," *Psychology Today* 7 (April 1974): 35–40.

19. K. Warner Schaie, "Toward a Stage Theory of Adult Cognitive Development," *International Journal of Aging and Human Development* 8 (1977–78).

20. The terms "undialectical progressivism" and "dialectical progressivism" are from Don Browning, *Generative Man* (New York: Dell, 1975), where they are utilized to describe alternative understandings of human development in psychoanalytic and neo-psychoanalytic thought.

21. Henri Nouwen and Walter Gaffney, *Aging: The Fulfillment of Life* (New York: Image Books, 1974), 79.

22. Ibid., 75.

23. William Clements, *Care and Counseling of the Aging* (Philadelphia: Fortress Press, 1979), 40–41.

24. Hans Loewald, *Psychoanalysis and the History of the Individual* (New Haven: Yale University Press, 1978), 22–23.

CHAPTER 5

1. Robert Butler, *Why Survive?* (New York: Harper & Row, 1975).
2. *Practical Works of Richard Baxter,* 4:399.
3. See, for example, Erik Erikson, *The Life Cycle Completed* (New York: W. W. Norton, 1982).
4. Lawrence Kohlberg, "Stages and Aging in Moral Development—Some Speculations," *The Gerontologist* 13 (Winter 1973): 500.
5. Gutmann, "Psychoanalysis and Aging," 496.
6. David L. Gutmann, "The Cross-Cultural Perspective: Notes Toward a Comparative Psychology of Aging," in *Handbook of the Psychology of Aging,* ed. James Birren and K. Warner Schaie (New York: D. Van Nostrand, 1977).
7. Gutmann, "Psychoanalysis and Aging," 494. See also D. Gutmann, J. Grunes, and B. Griffen, "The Clinical Psychology of Later Life," in *Transitions in Aging,* ed. N. Datan and N. Lohmann (New York: Academic Press, 1980).
8. Rebecca Cohen, Bertram Cohler, and Sidney Weissmann, eds., *Parenthood* (New York: Guilford Press, 1984), 3.
9. Lieberman and Tobin, *The Experience of Old Age.*
10. Heinz Kohut, *The Analysis of the Self* (New York: International Universities Press, 1972).
11. Bertram Cohler, "Autonomy and Interdependence in the Family of Adulthood: A Psychological Perspective," *The Gerontologist* 23 (February 1983): 33–39.
12. Robert Butler and Myrna Lewis, *Aging and Mental Health,* 3d ed. (St. Louis: C. V. Mosby, 1982), 36.
13. Ibid.
14. Robert Butler, "The Life Review: An Interpretation of Reminiscence in the Aged," *Psychiatry* 26 (1963): 65–76.
15. Lieberman and Tobin, *The Experience of Old Age,* 309.
16. Erik Erikson, "Reflections on Dr. Borg's Life Cycle," in *Adulthood,* ed. Erik Erikson (New York: W. W. Norton, 1978), 26.
17. Ibid., 12.
18. Calvin, *Commentaries,* 2:37.
19. Bridge, "A Word to the Aged," 186.
20. Parker Palmer, *The Company of Strangers* (New York: Crossroad, 1981), 77.
21. Gutmann, "The Cross-Cultural Perspective," 316.

CHAPTER 6

1. Robert Gray and David Moberg, *The Church and the Older Person,* rev. ed. (Grand Rapids: Wm. B. Eerdmans, 1977), 188.
2. Charles Taylor, "Understanding in Human Science," *Review of Metaphysics* 34 (September 1980): 25–38.
3. See Bernstein's discussion of the Cartesian Anxiety in *Beyond Objectivism and Relativism,* 16–20.

4. See Browning, *Religious Ethics and Pastoral Care.*
5. Schleiermacher, *Soliloquies,* 98–99.
6. Bridge, "A Word to the Aged," 189.
7. Thomas, "Age and Authority in Early Modern England."
8. A helpful annotated biblography of this literature is found in McKee, ed., *Philosophical Foundations of Gerontology,* 81–84.
9. Bernice Neugarten, Robert Havighurst, and Sheldon Tobin, "The Measurement of Life Satisfaction," in *Aging in America,* ed. Cary Kart and Barbara Manard (New York: Alfred Publishing, 1976).
10. Ibid., 124.
11. Ibid., 132.
12. Ibid.
13. Ibid., 133.
14. David Gutmann, "Observations on Culture and Mental Health in Later Life," in *Handbook of Mental Health and Aging,* ed. James Birren and R. B. Sloane (Englewood Cliffs, N.J.: Prentice-Hall, 1980), 429–47.
15. Ibid., 443.
16. Erikson, *The Life Cycle Completed,* 64–65.
17. Erik Erikson, *Childhood and Society,* rev. ed. (New York: W. W. Norton, 1964), 268.
18. Erik Erikson, *Identity and the Life Cycle* (New York: International Universities Press, 1959), 104.
19. Erik Erikson, *Insight and Responsibility* (New York: W. W. Norton, 1964), 133.
20. P. S. Timiras, *Developmental Physiology and Aging* (New York: John Wiley & Sons, 1970), 324.
21. James Birren, "Progress in Research on Aging in the Behavioral and Social Sciences," *Human Development* 23 (1980): 33–45.
22. David Barash, *Sociobiology and Behavior* (New York: Elsevier, 1977).
23. A discussion of certain issues related to this point may be found in Edward Shils, "Tradition and the Generations: On the Difficulties of Transmission," *The American Scholar* 53 (Winter 1983/84): 27–40.
24. A helpful discussion of programming possibilities in ministry with older adults is Donald F. Clingan, *Aging Persons in the Community of Faith,* new rev. ed. (St. Louis: Christian Board of Publication, 1980).
25. Ogden, *Faith and Freedom,* 85.

CHAPTER 7

1. Robert C. Neville, *Reconstruction of Thinking* (Albany: State University of New York Press, 1981), 19.
2. Ibid., 21.
3. Clements, *Care and Counseling of the Aging,* 24.
4. Ogden, *Faith and Freedom,* 85.
5. Cotton Mather, *A Good Old Age: A Brief Essay on the Glory of Aged Piety* (Boston, 1726), 8.

6. Johann Baptist Metz, *Faith in History and Society* (New York: Seabury, 1980).

7. Erikson, *The Life Cycle Completed*, 62.

8. See Fischer, *Growing Old in America*.

9. Claus Westermann, *Blessing in the Bible and the Life of the Church* (Philadelphia: Fortress Press, 1978), 5.

10. Ibid., 65.

11. Ibid., 5.

12. The term "values" is notoriously ambiguous and multifaceted. I am using the term to refer to all those things that lead to or enhance, in Westermann's meaning, "well-being." As I am using it, then, values may be either moral or nonmoral (but not, I hope it is clear from my usage, immoral).

13. Westermann, *Blessing,* 93.

14. William James, *Pragmatism and the Meaning of Truth* (Cambridge: Harvard University Press, 1978), 143.

15. Charles Hartshorne, *Man's Vision of God* (Chicago: Open Court, 1941), 117.

16. Ogden, *Faith and Freedom*, 83.

17. Gordon Jackson, *Pastoral Care and Process Theology* (Washington, D.C.: University Press of America, 1981), 82–83.

18. Westermann, *Blessing,* 117.